Springer Series

FOCUS ON WOMEN

Violet Franks, Ph.D., Series Editor

Confronting the major psychological, medical, and social issues of today and tomorrow, *Focus on Women* provides a wide range of books on the changing concerns of women.

VOLUME 1
THE SAFETY OF FERTILITY CONTROL
Editor-in-Chief: Louis G. Keith, M.D.
Associate Editors: Deryck R. Kent, M.D., Gary S. Berger, M.D., and Janelle R. Brittain, M.B.A.

VOLUME 2
THERAPY WITH WOMEN
A Feminist Philosophy of Treatment
Susan Sturdivant, Ph.D.

VOLUME 3
SHELTERING BATTERED WOMEN
A National Study and Service Guide
Albert R. Roberts, D.S.W.

VOLUME 4
WOMEN OVER FORTY
Visions and Realities
Marilyn R. Block, Ph.D., Janice L. Davidson, M.S., and Jean D. Grambs, Ed.D.

VOLUME 5
THE STEREOTYPING OF WOMEN
Its Effects on Mental Health
Violet Franks, Ph.D. and Esther D. Rothblum, Ph.D.

VOLUME 6
THE BATTERED WOMAN SYNDROME
Lenore E. Walker, Ed.D.

VOLUME 7
WOMEN THERAPISTS WORKING WITH WOMEN
New Theory and Process of Feminist Therapy
Claire M. Brody, Ph.D., Editor

CLAIRE M. BRODY, Ph.D., is Adjunct Associate Professor in the Department of Psychology, Sociology and Anthropology of the College of Staten Island, City University of New York. In addition to teaching and counseling at the City University over the last 17 years, she has also taught at Fairleigh Dickinson University and Long Island University and has been a school psychologist and a therapist with mental health clinics in New York and New Jersey. She is a Diplomate of the American Board of Professional Psychology and has written articles and papers in the fields of college counseling and teaching, as well as psychotherapy with women. She received her doctoral degree in psychology from New York University.

Women Therapists Working with Women

New Theory and Process of Feminist Therapy

Claire M. Brody, Ph.D.
Editor

Foreword by Florence L. Denmark, Ph.D.

Springer Publishing Company
New York

Springer Publishing Company, Inc.
200 Park Avenue South
New York, New York 10003

84 85 86 87 88 / 10 9 8 7 6 5 4 3 2 1

Library of Congress Cataloging in Publication Data

Main entry under title:
Women therapists working with women.
  (Springer series, focus on women; v. 7)
  Includes bibliographies and index.
  1. Feminist therapy.   2. Women psychotherapists.   3. Women—Mental health.
I. Brody, Claire M.   II. Series.
RC489.F45W67   1984   616.89'14088042   84-10516
ISBN 0-8261-4550-7

Printed in the United States of America

To My Mother
Anna Hudesman
1894–1979
and
My Granddaughter
Anna Rivka Perlmutter
Born July 6, 1982

". . . this composite of archetypes . . .
this child, this little girl, had
found the materials for her dreams
in the rubbish heaps of our old
civilisation, had found them,
worked on them, and in spite of
everything had made her images of
herself come to life . . ."

Doris Lessing
The Memoirs of a Survivor

Contents

Foreword

It was in the early part of the twentieth century when Freud revolutionalized people's thinking about the mind and emotions and developed a method of therapy for unhappy ("sick") people. While saying that his method was "value-free" and based on immutable laws of human behavior, he, as we know, was mirroring his Victorian world. That world, unhappily still much with us, includes the conscious and unconscious notion that women are not *ever* truly well, that the female condition is, somehow, innately pathologic, and that to even try to become "well" only puts women in a more severe pathologic state.

This notion is carried forward by such eminent writers and scientists as Erikson, whose poorly controlled study "proved" that females and males reasoned differently because of their anatomical differences.

Men's and women's illnesses have been sex-typed; what is appropriately feminine (such as depression) is seen as much more pathologic when seen in men, particularly by male therapists.

Since Freud's entrance nearly a century ago, many therapies have been instituted. Some, such as his traditional psychoanalysis and analytically oriented psychotherapy, rely on investigation of intrapsychic processes. Others, some quite recent, such as behavior therapy, implosion, European imagery, and the so-called client-centered therapies, utilize intrapsychic processes and/or responses to the environment. While these more recently recognized therapies have gained sanction as a response to a need for something other than traditional psychoanalysis, they nonetheless generally mirror the prevailing ideology of sex-typed pathology.

In addition to the notions that unhappy people are "sick" and that this pathology is sex-typed is the general belief that the therapist is all-knowing and thus all-powerful. The person who seeks therapeutic help is in a position of dependency. For women, who are generally in a state of dependency, this role which they must assume is not therapeutic—it reinforces the power relationships to which they have been subjected all of their lives.

It may be seen that most types of therapy involve (1) values and (2) power. The values and power of the client ("sick person") are subjugated to those of the therapist.

Feminist therapy—what this book is about—is something different. It is not about power, but about equality. It is not about values, mine and yours, but about values in a changing world. It does not pretend to be value-free, because not only *can't* it be, it *must not* be.

Feminist therapy is relatively new and has grown as feminism itself has grown. It is no coincidence that the growth of one parallels the growth of the other.

Feminist therapy is seen against a backdrop of our culture. It is the process of helping women to understand themselves as alive, thinking, feeling persons in a rapidly changing world full of contradictions. While the majority of psychotherapy clients are women, few of the extant therapeutic methods take into account gender-role norms that discriminate against women. Feminist therapy has at its root the idea that females and males should be equal in opportunities for gaining power—personal, economic, and political.

Claire Brody has done a great service by bringing together a collection of papers by outstanding writers and organizing them in a format which covers the topic of feminist therapy in a way which is thoughtful and logical.

Brody's book is positive, just as the subject itself is positive. She examines the historical underpinnings of the female condition with the social forces which provide external stress. She shows how feminist therapy does not use the notion of the environment to take away individual responsibility. Instead, her examination shows how an understanding of the environment can provide the means for coping, rather *living*, responsibly, positively, and freely.

Brody has taken care to look at the broad issues and—no small task—to examine the specific concerns against the general milieu.

The theoretical papers which discuss the broad concerns of feminist therapy are sound and cogent. The external obstacles which stand in the way of women's access to power—sex-role stereotypes, power struggles, issues particularly relevant to minority women, math anxiety—are thoughtfully and positively dealt with. The papers discussing therapy itself should be read by all therapists, women and men, in order for them to develop new strategies for helping clients. These papers offer insights for all therapists who may use sex-typed responses to their clients of both genders.

As Brody illustrates, feminist therapy has developed in a short period of time to be a unified method of treatment for women having difficulties coping with their lives. What is gratifying, in addition, is to read the papers by a number of thoughtful, knowledgeable writers who have added their own individual analyses and perceptions to the subject as a whole. This exemplifies feminist therapy. It is a way to allow women to be themselves with their individual thoughts, perceptions, and values and teaches them to be free and responsible human beings.

Florence L. Denmark, Ph.D.
Professor of Psychology
Hunter College and the
Graduate Center of the
City University of New York

Acknowledgments

To the many people who contributed to the birthing of this book, I want to extend my thanks:

Violet Franks, Editor of the Springer Focus on Women Series, who, from the first, was supportive, positive, and encouraging about the importance of bringing these ideas together.

My daughters, Jessica, Laura, and Naomi, for their editorial and technical assistance with all phases of editing this volume as well as with my own chapters.

Patterson Smith, my publisher friend, for his literary counsel and aid in helping me say what I want, better!

Thomas Kelly, bibliophile, for his invaluable assistance with the Index.

Edwin Kasin, Elizabeth Beck, Jayne Mangino, Carmel Friedman, Nancy Boyd Franklin, Belinda Williams, Frances Trotman—all of whom read my own chapters and offered cogent comments on content and style of presentation.

The members of the Women Therapists Group who, singly and together, were the inspiration for formulating the concept of therapist as group model, and who helped lessen my lingering imposter feelings. I want to mention one member especially, Eve Cohen, whose insights affected us all and whose untimely death left a deeply felt gap in the group.

Alex Brody, whose steadfast concern, involvement, and patience have probably contributed the most toward facilitating the pursuit and completion of this project.

Claire M. Brody

Contributors

Jessica Benjamin is in private practice in New York City. In addition, she has been engaged in research on mother–infant interaction at the Albert Einstein College of Medicine, where she was a Fellow in psychiatry. She is the author of numerous articles on psychoanalysis, feminism, and social theory, including "Master and Slave" in *Powers of Desire*. She is currently completing a book on the psychology of sexual domination. She received her Ph.D. in sociology at New York University and has trained at the Postdoctoral Institute for Psychotherapy and Psychoanalysis there.

Pauline Rose Clance is Associate Professor of Psychology at Georgia State University in Atlanta, and in part-time private practice. With Suzanne Imes, she wrote the article on the "Imposter Phenomenon in High Achieving Women," in *Psychotherapy* in 1978. Her therapeutic orientation is gestalt-existential. Her research interests include women and achievement, intimate systems, and body awareness. She is past-President of the Southeastern Psychological Association. She received her Ph.D. in psychology from the University of Kentucky.

Irene Deitch is an Associate Professor of Psychology at the College of Staten Island of the City University of New York. She also has a part-time private practice on Staten Island. A past president of the

Richmond County (N.Y.) Psychological Association, she was the recipient last year of a "Women Helping Women" award sponsored by Soroptimists International. She earned her Ph.D. in psychology from Yeshiva University as an "older adult returning to college." She has participated in workshops and symposia on feminist issues, and presentꝫd papers on math anxiety in women.

Luise Eichenbaum is co-founder with Susie Orbach of the Women's Therapy Centre Institute in New York and the Women's Therapy Centre in London. As a practicing psychotherapist, she is involved in the postgraduate training of other mental health practitioners. She has given lectures and seminars on the subject of women and mental health throughout the United Kingdom. She is the co-author, with Susie Orbach, of *What Do Women Want: Exploding the Myth of Dependency* and *Understanding Women: A Feminist Psychoanalytic Approach* (published in the United Kingdom as *Outside In . . . Inside Out*).

Iris Fodor is a Professor in the Department of Educational Psychology at New York University where she trains school psychologists. At N.Y.U. she is also a member of the Women's Studies Commission, which has developed a program for women in the human services. She is a therapist who has lectured and written extensively about women's issues and mental health. She has a Ph.D. from Boston University.

Margaret S. Gibbs is Professor of Psychology at Fairleigh Dickinson University in New Jersey and a Diplomate of the American Board of Professional Psychology. Her work includes teaching, clinical practice, and research. She is co-editor of *Community Psychology: Theoretical and Empirical Approaches* and *Psychopathology of Childhood*. Her doctorate is in clinical psychology, from Harvard University.

Suzanne Imes is a psychotherapist in private practice in Atlanta, Georgia. She also supervises graduate students in psychotherapy. With Pauline Clance, she originated the imposter phenomenon theory, which they first described in 1978 in *Psychotherapy: Theory, Research and Practice*. In her therapy work with adults, she focuses on body–mind relationships and uses a gestalt approach to intimate systems. She is past-President of the Division of Women Psychologists of the Georgia

Psychological Association. She received her Ph.D. in clinical psychology from Georgia State University.

Debra R. Kaufman is currently Associate Professor of Sociology in the Department of Sociology and Anthropology at Northeastern University, Boston, Massachusetts and the coordinator of the Women's Studies Program there. She has authored numerous articles on the family, sex roles, occupations, and the professions. She is co-author of *Achievement and Women: Challenging the Assumptions*. She has her Ph.D. from Cornell University.

Susie Orbach is co-founder with Luise Eichenbaum of the Women's Therapy Centre in London and the Women's Therapy Centre Institute in New York. As a practicing psychotherapist, she is involved in the postgraduate training of mental health practitioners and has given lectures and seminars on the subjects of women and mental health throughout the United Kingdom. She is the co-author, with Luise Eichenbaum, of *What Do Women Want: Exploring the Myth of Dependency; Understanding Women: A Feminist Psychoanalytic Approach;* and author of *Fat Is a Feminist Issue* and *Fat Is a Feminist Issue II*.

Esther D. Rothblum is Assistant Professor of Psychology at the University of Vermont in Burlington. She previously worked in the Depression Research Unit at Yale University. She is the author of numerous papers and has conducted workshops and symposia on depression and women's mental health and is co-chair of the Feminist Research Committee of the Association for Women in Psychology. She is also co-author with Violet Franks of Volume 5 in the Springer series Focus on Women, *The Stereotyping of Women: Its Effects on Mental Health*. She received her Ph.D. in psychology from Rutgers University.

Barbara Cohn Schlachet is an Adjunct Clinical Supervisor in Graduate Psychology at Yeshiva University and a Clinical Supervisor at the Institute for Contemporary Psychotherapy in New York City. She is also a practicing psychoanalyst. She has written articles on rapid intervention with families in crisis; violence in the family; and the theory and practice of feminist therapy. She has her Ph.D. in psychology from New York University.

Laura J. Solomon is an Assistant Professor in the Department of Psychology at the University of Vermont in Burlington. She previously worked as a consultant in Washington, D.C., developing health-related interventions on a national level. She has authored papers on stress management, health behavior change, and women's issues. She recently co-edited a book entitled *Marketing Health Behavior*. She received her doctorate in psychology from Virginia Polytechnic Institute and State University.

Frances K. Trotman is founder and Director of the Contemporary Counseling and Psychotherapy Institute in Teaneck, New Jersey, and is also in private practice. A high school guidance counselor prior to becoming a psychologist, she has published several articles on race and IQ. She holds a Ph.D. in counseling psychology from Columbia University.

Rhoda Kesler Unger is Professor of Psychology at Montclair State College in New Jersey, and is a Fellow of the American Psychological Association. She is co-author with Florence Denmark of *Woman: Dependent or Independent Variable?*; author of *Female and Male: Psychological Perspectives*; and co-editor of the forthcoming book *Women, Gender and Social Psychology*. She has authored over 20 articles and book chapters on sex stereotyping, interpersonal perception, helping, and social power. She has a Ph.D. in experimental psychology from Harvard University.

Florence L. Denmark, who wrote the Foreword to this book, is Professor of Psychology at Hunter College and the Graduate Center of the City University of New York. She is former President of the American Psychological Association, and of Division 35, the Division of the Psychology of Women. She was also President of the New York State Psychological Association. She is a recognized scholar and the author of many articles related to the psychology of women. Among her published books are *Woman: Dependent or Independent Variable*, with Rhoda Unger; *Psychology of Woman: Future Directions in Research*, co-edited and authored with Julia Sherman; *Woman*, Volume I (Editor); and co-author of the recently published book, *Women's Choices, Women's Realities*. She has a Ph.D. in social psychology from the University of Pennsylvania.

Introduction

CLAIRE M. BRODY

This volume is a collection of innovative papers on the theory and process of an evolving specialty, feminist psychotherapy. It is nearly ten years since Violet Franks and Vasanti Burtle gathered together a group of therapists to write about the changing world of the women with whom they worked. In their book, *Women in Therapy* (1974), they suggested that therapists and their women clients would have to scrutinize new role options. Since then, there have been a number of books and countless articles written, and this volume provides a cross section of some emerging themes.

When I was young, I was very preoccupied with acquiring independence. I needed to separate myself from my mother, a woman of dominating character, and I could only imagine acquiring independence by going as far away from home as possible. Later, when I became a parent, one of my daughters also needed to go as far away as possible; another, in her ambivalence, resisted going with all her energies. These are two strategies of adolescents that Maggie Scarf (1980) points to in *Unfinished Business*. Teaching women to come to terms with their independence is a goal for women therapists in therapy and a major theme of this book.

In 1979 I helped edit the reminiscences of my mother (Hudesman, 1979), who was then 85 and had never published anything before. She was an early feminist and union organizer, and though she had been writing her recollections, observations of the world and people, and philosophical musings for more than 60 years, she had never shared them with anyone because she mistrusted her writing ability. While engaged in going through the boxes of her writings, it occurred to me that I, too, had never trusted my literary or creative efforts, even though I had a similarly strong drive to share my thoughts. I particularly wanted to write about the psychotherapy I was doing with women. I was one of those who, despite evidence of achievement, always felt as though I were fooling everyone. About this time I read Pauline Clance and Suzanne Imes' (1978) seminal article and realized that I was a victim of the "imposter phenomenon." This becomes another theme of this book.

Each of the papers in this book deals with some facet of working with women. The first section, Therapists as Women, delineates feminist therapy theory. Imparting values in treatment and being authentic are basic questions raised in my opening paper, "Authenticity in Feminist Therapy." Which values to impart and how best to do this without intruding on the treatment process is discussed.

"The Therapist as Imposter," by Margaret Gibbs, introduces contingent reinforcement as a concept of significance to women assuaging their fraudulent feelings. Gibbs suggests, however, that imposter feelings are probably sex-blind and are a built-in construct for practitioners of most theories of psychotherapy. She also delineates the role conflict for women therapists, who are inclined to use "expressivity" as compared to "instrumentality" in their approach.

Before reading the position papers of the second section of the book, Feminism and Psychoanalysis, it would be important to recognize that psychoanalytic therapy in an arena of feminism is both anachronistic and revolutionary! In *Unfinished Business* Scarf has said that from earliest infancy females more than males seem conditioned to respond and react to humans. This suggests an innately stronger "other people" bias, which is enhanced in female children through cultural training to make them caregivers. At the same time women must deal from girlhood on with those contradictory messages that push them toward independence and meaningful work. The most poetic joining of psychoanalysis and feminism appeared in Dorothy Dinnerstein's book, *The Mermaid and the Minotaur* (1976). She foreshadowed a new theory of feminist therapy that helps women restructure their traditional relationships and gender-based work roles vis-à-vis men. The roots of a woman's jealousy, Dinnerstein explains, are in her female-dominated early childhood, but the traditional oedipal symbolism is an oversimplification of the sex-role education that takes place from age two to five (p. 2).

The authors in the second section reinterpret traditional psychoanalytic developmental theory. Jessica Benjamin's article on "The Convergence of Psychoanalysis and Feminism" reflects Dinnerstein's belief when she says that we must, as women, free ourselves from a male conception of autonomy and refocus the oedipal issues and social gender roles. She makes a case for rethinking the polarization of gender development, suggesting that "we must not assume the old ideal of autonomy in our struggle for liberation, and we must not defend the old restriction of femininity to nurturing at the price of self-assertion."

Luise Eichenbaum and Susie Orbach in their paper "Feminist Psychoanalysis" address the issue of "how feminist concerns reshape the terrain on which psychological enquiry is based." They describe the evolution of a girl's relationship with her mother and ascribe to this shaping experience the later difficulty women have with separation, autonomy, and emotional nurturance. They explain how feminist psychoanalysis, with its unconventional emphasis on the importance of the therapist–client relationship, enables the woman to deal with her newfound entitlements.

The style of psychoanalytic therapy conducted by women is distinguished from that of male therapists in Barbara Cohn Schlachet's paper, "Female Role Socialization: The Analyst and the Analysis." She attributes female therapists' style to the fact that women have learned historically to relate to one another "out of a sense of continuity and shared experience." She also refers to the therapy literature that confirms the therapeutic efficacy of the greater degree of self-disclosure and modeling by women in their psychoanalytically framed treatment.

In the third section of the book, Feminist Therapy: Treatment Strategies, several key issues in feminist therapy are opened for discussion, among them, how women deal with success and achievement. Scarf has said that a prevalent theme in women's fantasies is loss, contrary to men's fantasies, where achievement motifs predominate. The women have a special vulnerability to losses in relationships, and their reaction of depression to problems is different, according to their life decade. In addition, their failure to adapt to shifts confronting them at turning points affects their sense of competence and limits their ability to accept accomplishment.

The lead article in this section is "Treatment of the Imposter Phenomenon in High-Achieving Women." It is the sequel to Suzanne Imes and Pauline Clance's original paper in which they defined the imposter phenomenon. Here they discuss specific strategies for working individually with clients who display one or more of the imposter phenomenon's characteristics. A major goal of the therapy is "empowerment," helping a woman develop a solid, realistic sense of her own capabilities. The imposter phenomenon is never viewed narrowly as a single symptom, however, but rather in the context of earlier family dynamics and societal expectations. The chapter includes a number of illuminating vignettes from actual cases.

In "Strategies for Dealing with Sex-Role Stereotypes," Iris Fodor and Esther Rothblum discuss three categories of female clients, focusing on representative disorders, while they suggest effective interventions that will decrease clinical symptoms of their disorders. They also maintain that feminist therapists need to consider prevention as well as intervention methods, and they stress the responsibility of feminist therapists for informing and educating mental health professionals about the influence of stereotypes in therapy.

Frances Trotman, writing about "Psychotherapy with Black Women," talks of the dual handicaps of racism and sexism in black women's development. She traces the ways in which the history of social practices for black women has paralleled or diverged from that of white women. She suggests that there is great complexity in changing a damaged feeling of self when this additional racial variable is present, and she points to the kinds of interventions that succeed or fail in her treatment of black females.

My article on "Feminist Therapy with Minority Clients" reflects my interest in cultural variables in therapy. I know that stereotypic problems sometimes affect minority women differently than they do white women and that some minority women change their lives only when the therapist-model is ethnically similar, a point which Trotman makes. In my experience, however, I have rarely found racial disparity to be a bar to success in treatment *with those women who do decide to work with me*. So I have written a paper which discusses this issue and presents some hypotheses for my successes. Luise Eichenbaum and Susie Orbach (1982) have told us that all therapies are informed by a political perspective. Some therapists avoid or are anxious about working with clients different from themselves. I discuss several possible reasons for this in the chapter.

Gender Issues is the last section of the book and focuses more broadly on issues related to women's psychology. Before discussing the chapters in this section, it is relevant to mention Brown and Liss-Levinson's chapter in Corsini's book (1981), which suggested that feminist therapy is based on the assumption that therapists will use the insights of political feminism to create "new strategies for intervention and new structures for service delivery" (p. 299). This concept is in contrast to therapy that derives its norm from cultural sexism.

Maracek, Kravetz & Finn (1979) defined feminist therapy as "neither a technique nor a system of therapy" but rather a "perspective to be applied to the theories, techniques and ethical standards of traditional therapies" (p. 734). Feminist therapists encourage clients to evaluate ways in which social roles and norms influence their personal experiences and to explore solutions that transcend tradition. It is important to know, as Maracek et al. point out, that the results of a study of 400 women showed that clients who identified themselves as members of the women's movement evaluated their feminist therapy as more helpful than traditional therapy; non members evaluated feminist and traditional therapies as equally helpful. The two groups of clients differed mainly in regard to political attitudes: clients of feminist therapists were more likely to describe their political views as radical, and to identify themselves as members of the women's movement, than clients of traditional therapists. There is a looser relationship between professional output (e.g., writings) and professional rewards (e.g., power) for women, than for men; if women are rewarded it is more often with prestige than with positions of actual power. These authors provide the background for the gender issues discussed by Rhoda Unger in the lead chapter in this section.

Rhoda Unger's chapter, "Hidden Assumptions in Theory and Research on Women," rigorously reviews the ideological assumptions and practices in feminist research and literature and concludes that there are biases that affect the answers about the sex-related reality for women.

In her chapter, "Working Women and Stress," Laura Solomon takes up the reasons for the aggravated stresses of some sociocultural groups of women. Lower socioeconomic class women who combine housewife and work roles are more stressed than their upper-class counterparts. Solomon offers treatment as well as environmental change options for women.

Irene Deitch, in reporting her innovative research, "A Feminist Approach to Math Anxiety Reduction," takes a feminist approach to the treatment of women with this problem. Deitch acknowledges that math anxiety and math avoidance are not unique to women and that the disorder is undoubtedly related to the socialization processes for both sexes. She has adopted a treatment approach that is especially valuable and relevant for women in changing their perception of themselves as potential achievers.

Debra Kaufman is concerned about women and their acquisition of power as a perquisite of their female identity. In her paper, "Some Feminist Concerns in an Age of Networking," she puts forth the idea that networking can begin to redress the imbalance of control and achievement between the sexes through counteracting the accumulated disadvantages of male-mentoring that women have had to rely on in the past.

We continue to live in a male-dominated society even though inroads have been made against the legal and emotional bases of male domination. Nancy Chodorow pointed out in *The Reproduction of Mothering* that women continue to marry and mother, and produce daughters with mothering capacities and desires. The inequality women experience in the labor force and in the family do not have to be enduring elements of their lives. Indeed, the view of women as unproductive and insignificant was not true historically, Chodorow notes, and this view is not an inevitable consequence of a women's mothering inclinations (1978, p. 6–7). The gender differences and inequities that persist in contemporary social organization are examined in this volume by feminist writers who present new theories and processes for dealing with the current reality, with the expectation that their work will contribute to changing it.

REFERENCES

Brown, L. S., & Liss-Levinson, N. Feminist therapy. I. In Raymond S. Corsini, (Ed.), *Handbook of innovative psychotherapies*. New York: Wiley, 1981, pp. 299–314.

Chodorow, N. *The reproduction of mothering: Psychoanalysis and the sociology of gender*. Berkeley, Calif.: University of California Press, 1978, pp. 6–7.

Clance, P., & Imes, S. The imposter phenomenon in high-achieving women: Dynamics and therapeutic intervention. *Psychotherapy: Theory, Research and Practice*, Fall 1978, 15 (3), 241–247.

Dinnerstein, D. *The mermaid and the minotaur: Sexual arrangements and sexual malaise*. New York: Harper & Row, 1976.

Eichenbaum, L., & Orbach, S. *Outside in . . . Inside out*. New York: Penguin Books, 1982.

Franks, V., & Burtle, V. (Eds.). *Women in therapy*. New York: Brunner/Mazel, 1974.

Hudesman, A. *Fourscore and five*. New York: Psychological Dimensions, 1979.

Maracek, J., Kravetz, D. & Finn, S. Comparison of women who enter feminist therapy and women who enter traditional therapy. *Journal of Consulting and Clinical Psychology*, August, 1979, 47 (4), 734–742.

Scarf, Maggie. *Unfinished business*. Garden City, N. Y.: Doubleday, 1980.

■ one
THERAPISTS AS WOMEN

■ 1

Authenticity in Feminist Therapy

CLAIRE M. BRODY

FEMINIST CONCEPTS OF PSYCHOTHERAPY

Elizabeth Williams, in *Notes of a Feminist Therapist* (1976), points out that by focusing attention on intrapsychic conflicts as the source of a woman's psychological distress, rather than on societal oppression and prejudice, most traditional therapists increase the woman's tendency to feel responsible for and therefore guilty about her own pain, further inhibiting her ability to change. Nevertheless, I can agree with Friedman (1980) that there is something in the separation and identification process between mothers and daughters that makes it difficult for a woman to achieve a sense of herself, and this early developmental relationship can be a fruitful realm of exploration in the therapy.

Female children are often given inadequate encouragement by their mothers for early independence, and separation from the mother can be more difficult for the girl than for the boy. Thus, the girl often does not learn as well how to cope independently with the environment; safety and effectiveness lie in affective, affiliative ties, not in achievement. As Hoffman (1972) pointed out, if the girl's mother shows an increase in anxiety as the child moves toward greater independence, then this is sufficient to make the child doubt her competence.

To understand a woman's lack of achievement in education or work I find it productive to analyze interpersonal variables. I believe that personality reflects the expectations of real or imagined people in the client's life. A variety of research projects in the 1970s showed that women's behavior generally still conforms to sex-role expectations. When women fail to act in role-appropriate ways, they run the risk of disapproval and outright hostility from others. This is reinforced from childhood by rewards and punishments and further reinforced by experienced social values. Qualities like competitiveness, aggressiveness, assertiveness, and competence are not unequally possessed by men by virtue of genetics, but come about in early socialization rituals and can be characteristic of both sexes in different situations, domestically or in the world of business (Darley, 1976; Miller, 1976).

Matina Horner (1972) postulated that women are motivated to avoid success and, furthermore, that the motive is acquired early in life in conjunction with sex-role standards. This motive may not be equally important for all women, but it can be aroused when they are in more personally competitive situations. Condry and Dyer (1976) pointed out that if men are inclined to put women down when they show signs of competence in something other than homemaking, a large part of this is due to what men project in the way of expectations from *their* upbringing. If women accept such treatment without protest, even altering their actions to respond to it, then they are reacting on the basis of what they have come to expect. Thus sex-typed behavior is maintained.

Women in the past have often preferred male therapists because they mistrusted women therapists as both authorities and people (Chesler, 1975). In feminist therapy the therapists's prior family and clinical experience can render her more aware of and sensitive to stereotyped sex roles (Hare-Mustin, 1978). If sexist values are learned from a therapist, a woman client will be discouraged from expressing assertion, independence, and power (Rawlings & Carter, 1977). If a therapist, male or female, can "help" a woman without simultaneously dominating her, as she must surely have been many times before, then a new variable has been added to the equation. In this respect there is a real advantage in a female over a male therapist. A woman does not so much need a male model who is different from earlier ones, because this often reinforces the value stereotype of a powerful, accepting male. Rather, she needs a woman who models the different kind of woman *she* can become, so that a woman can be freed from minority-group traits and can supplant them with an image of competency without thinking she has to play the role of superwoman.

A woman who chooses to combine a career and motherhood often confronts an ambiguous situation. Despite the fact that the male member of the couple appears to offer free choice to his spouse, it is seldom so clear-cut to the woman; it is easier to be found "good" in the traditional role and a failure in occupational or professional achievement. The woman could, theoretically, compare her performance to relevant others—*if* they could be found. The woman therapist is often the first model that is authentic and available. The therapeutic relationship, where some semblance of equality is emphasized, may be the first life experience where a woman gets different feedback from a significant other: if she's lucky, from a woman therapist. In a period of rapid social change, the socially disadvantaged person (woman) will be most vulnerable and the female therapist can have a unique opportunity to affect the woman's feelings about herself.

Ruth Moulton, writing about Clara Thompson (Moulton, 1974), said that Thompson was aware of how hard it is for women to free themselves from old stereotypes and role expectations, and Thompson could accept their failure to do so without condescension. She explained that the therapist has to help women "disregard the backward pull exerted by parents, peers, husbands who may give lip service to a new freedom of choice for women but unwittingly add to their difficulties in achieving it" (Strouse, 1974, p. 286). Femininity cannot be defined simply by outer behavior, i.e., by carrying out of roles. The roles may change—a woman may be an architect, an administrator, roles previously held by men—but her self-image, her inner feelings about herself, may or may not be feminine. The woman's strength or lack of it in resisting the imposition of a social stereotype depends on the security of her self-definition (Menaker, 1974).

Delk and Ryan (1977) discuss the possible relationship between the type of personality of a therapist and the degree of stereotyping to which each type is prone. The ability of the therapist to help a woman become self-actualized may be more related to personality variables and the matching of these between therapist and client than just to the gender of the therapist, as was assumed previously by many feminist therapists. Personality characteristics which appear to carry the most weight are functions of feeling bound by cultural traditions and values and the degree of structure in the approach. This matter was also dealt with by Mogul (1982), who concluded that the impact of the therapist's gender on the outcome of treatment is related to many variables, for instance the client's developmental level, early relationships with parents, specific conflictual areas, *as well as the therapist's sensitivity and value system regarding gender issues* (emphasis added). Mogul says that conclusions about optimal client–therapist matches based on gender alone are therefore not warranted.

AUTHENTICITY IN THEORY

There have been a spate of studies pointing to the importance of the therapist's personality (Berger, 1974; Delk & Ryan, 1977; Bent, Putnam, Kiesler & Nowicki, 1976) and the effectiveness of therapist self-disclosure for outcome of therapy (Anchor, Strassberg, & Elkins, 1976; Kaslow, Cooper, & Linsenberg, 1979). Kaslow et al. focused it best in saying "a therapist's authenticity can add a new dimension to the interaction. The therapist can offer a significant contribution by sharing her personality, life style, values and verbalized assumptions while remaining flexible, open and undefensive" (p. 190).

Bugental (1965) described authenticity as the central concern of psychotherapy, as a primary existential value. His early definition of authenticity is still applicable: clarifying emotional needs through learning and experience, not merely learning to adjust to conditions. The therapist's revelation of true feelings, selective sharing of experiences, and undefensive presentation of a less than perfect authority stance can be frightening for a client who has had prior treatment with a more traditional, psychoanalytically oriented therapist who presented a more masked or mechanized format. This approach can also be a startling relief, however, and an impetus to new growth and the development of a better sense of self. Anchor, Strassberg, and Elkins (1976) report that therapist effectiveness is not necessarily related to the therapist's low level of self-disclosure—a traditional psychoanalytic notion. Rather, effective therapists are "capable of spontaneity, reveal their three-dimensionality, and implicitly invite their clients to learn through a credible model" (p. 158). For the therapist to be a significant force in a group or, for that matter, in individual therapy, there needs to be democratic regard, trust, and humanness (Berger, 1974). It is necessary to stress equality and authenticity in the relationship between the therapist and client, and this is especially important where a female therapist is modeling a projected autonomous role for a female client.

AUTHENTICITY IN PRACTICE

In response to the report of the APA Task Force on Sex Bias and Sex-Role Stereotyping in Psychotherapeutic Practice (1975), I have been reviewing my thinking about how I communicate values and influence the gender roles of clients, especially women. I work with women who are mostly in their twenties and thirties, who have been diagnosed as phobic or depressed. In couple therapy as well as in individual therapy, they often come to treatment with confusion or conflict about their identity. More often than not, their tentative efforts to break out of stereotyped, sex-typed roles with their spouses have met with negative consequences: their move to go to work or back to school was demeaned, directly or indirectly. A question that is often explored in individual treatment is the degree to which their femininity and/or adjustment as a woman is related to an early developmentally acquired self-image or to later social influences.

My own values about roles of women and men, both within marriage and in a variety of single life styles, are obviously the result of *my* accumulated familial attitudes and experiences. I assume that consciously or unconsciously these values will be involved in the therapy I do. I try to keep aware of how and when my values can be interwoven more effectively with the therapy. I do this overtly while I also have developed a more sensitive "third ear" for gender stereotypes (Brody, 1981). Marilyn Johnson (1976), studying women in group therapy with a feminist orientation, and Rachel Hare-Mustin (1978), in feminist family therapy, also make a plea for better definition of how values are transmitted in treatment.

Where it is relevant for a particular client, I have no hesitation in using myself as a model, since I expect to be modeled. The more important thing is for me to remain open to differences in the ultimate model that a client chooses for herself. This is especially important in my own practice because I treat women of diverse cultural, social, and class orientations. (See Chapter 9, "Feminist Therapy with Minority Clients.") LoPiccolo and Herman (1977) have pointed out that the psychotherapist's view of personality is influenced and shaped by the dominant elements in his or her anxiety. This anxiety can be triggered, in turn, by a nonspecific guilt related to culture, class, or racial discrimination the client has suffered. If, as a result, I "try too hard," I leave the client less choice about responding or not to my efforts. There is always the danger that the therapist's culturally valued behavior may become synonymous with mental health at the expense of the client's individual needs. While I acknowledge this risk,

I make new values sound possible without exploiting the clients and without assigning any immediate expectation for them.

What values do I want to convey to women—and to men? I value the complexity of my life, the fact that I can be competent at traditionally feminine, nurturing functions—cooking, handwork, childrearing—but also productive, energetic, going after what I want in the same way men have done. I transmit these values implicitly and explicitly, i.e., I model and disclose these traits and also convey, sometimes unconsciously, that I approve of them, at the same time that a woman is not expected to be like me in order to get approval.

For example, with female clients, I consider how they are affected by the men in their lives; with male clients, by the women in theirs. I will give you vignettes of four different women and one man in my practice, all in their 30's (names and life details changed.)

1. Evelyn: parent, housewife, she typifies "the Mad Housewife" (from the movie by that name). Her husband is the stereotype of a male chauvinist. Evelyn is unable to break out of this role. She comes to therapy very depressed, frigid, angry, and playing a passive role in the marriage. With Evelyn, I have said, "You *must* be angry. Is the sexual problem your fault? Your husband says it is. What will happen if you refuse to be demeaned, get mad?"

2. Ann: parent, housewife, now part-time student. She started out feeling locked into the stereotype of parent-housewife. She came into therapy with psychosomatic symptoms. She had affairs, and then found her earlier problem of sexual frigidity had changed, but not her marital relationship because her husband did not change. With Ann, I have said, "Speak up! You can demand help with the housework, and that your husband spend more time at home with you. You need to be clearer about what you want for *you*."

3. Pam: married, no children (husband's choice). She has focused her life on her career and on other men outside of marriage. Husband is weak but resistive to altering his patterns even in the face of increasing threats from wife to leave. Sex is satisfactory for wife with other men but less so with husband. With Pam, I have said, "What is the problem in leaving; what are you afraid of? What patterns were you repeating in your extramarital affairs?"

4. Cheryl: divorced; combines career and graduate school. She now lives alone, but wants marriage and children. She has many left-over dependencies and ambivalences about her underlying need to

"lean." She keeps finding immature men who are not ready for intimacy. She has good sexual relationships but feels "no one will ever care for me or take care of me." With Cheryl, I have said, "Why do you want children? Can you imagine being happy if you remain alone, with your career? Do you *need* to be taken care of?"

5. John: married, one child. His wife is the counterpart of Evelyn, the parent-housewife. He claims she would like to go back to work or school, but she never quite formulates the plan. With John, I have said, "What are your expectations for yourself in your family; in your male sex role? What would you fear if your wife changed; what is your stake in the status quo? What might you be doing, unconsciously, to keep your wife in the role she is in?"

In each case, my questions reflect my values. Total objectivity is of course impossible for any therapist, but perhaps especially for women, who are never so emanicipated that they cannot get caught in a web of defensiveness about *their* unsolved sexism problems. Gloria Gottsegen[1] said, "a woman therapist's attitudes toward her sex, her sexuality, aging, authority, dependence, risk-taking, the women's movement, and her clients are, by implication, issues that will affect her work with the opposite sex." Nevertheless, I have found that although one might reasonably expect that I would be more sensitive to clients who are struggling with problems that I continue to deal with in my own life, the fact of the matter is that I can be most clear about my values with women who are furthest away from where I have ever been, for example divorced or single young women and single young men.

An interesting side issue that Berger (1974) discusses and with which I concur is that as I grow older, I, too, tend to become more actively confronting with clients, less passive. To be involved, to use myself as a variable in the process, entails using, from time to time, mimicry, provocation, joking, annoyance, analogies, or brief lectures. It also means utilizing my own and others' physical behavior, sensations, emotional states, and reactions to me and others, and sharing a variety of intuitive responses. This is being authentic. It may be why, since my early training days, I have been a particularly successful therapist with young schizophrenic clients.

1. Gloria Behar Gottsegen in her Introduction to the Symposium, Counter-transference issues in women therapists. APA Annual Convention, Washington, D.C., 1976.

A similar hypothesis, that therapist characteristics are crucial in the outcome of treatment with schizophrenics, was made by Whitehorn and Betz (1960). They found that the more successful therapists manifested initiative in inquiry, expressed honest disagreement, challenged the client's deprecatory attitudes, set realistic limits for acceptable behavior, and participated actively in the treatment process, including using self as an example. All of these traits are critical to establishing myself as an authentic person.

I have treated one woman client, age 44, at two different crisis periods of her life, about 10 years apart. Both crises entailed depression, inhibition of affect, and superdependency on family members. She struggled with a deep-seated fear of fulfilling herself and with the demands of intimacy. Before she could see me as an accepting peer, one whose life style apparently had many facets she could model, she needed first to work through her guilt and rage from an earlier family drama, full of double messages from her mother about achievement and independence. In discussing the evolution and importance of the mother–daughter bond in the therapeutic process, Friedman (1980) points out that the bond that arises, by comparison, between the client and the therapist can be experienced differently; it does not have to be severed to achieve autonomy, as in the earlier parent–child relationship. Rather, it is a new kind of connection that can be fostered and can eventually lead to a consolidation of the client's psychological strengths, with emerging independence.

The concept of double bind is very appropriate in describing the experience of women in this society who have been trapped and systematically driven crazy because making choices within the confines of what they are told simultaneously to do and not to do denies a part of their real life experience (Kaschak, 1976). Women decide, more often than not, that there is something wrong with *them*. The psychotherapy *of* women, *by* women, more than anything else should include active sharing by the therapist of her experiences as a woman-person in this society. In her modeling role, the therapist demystifies "women" in that characteristics traditionally and untraditionally ascribed to women are validated and valued, and a fully functioning woman is seen as not just a caricature of a man. The therapist and the client become joint forces of change in the client's life, within the therapeutic context.

I am reminded of Doris Lessing, the British novelist, of her idealistic valuing of originality and innovation even in the face of society's disapproval. She says, perhaps a little ingenuously, in the Preface to *The Golden Notebook* that we must tell every child as she grows up:

You are in the process of being indoctrinated. We have not yet evolved a system of education that is not indoctrination. What you are taught is an amalgam of current prejudice and the choices of this particular culture . . . you are being taught by the people who have been able to accommodate themselves to a regime of thought laid down by predecessors. Those of you who are more robust and individualistic than others will be encouraged to leave and find your own ways of educating your judgement (Lessing, 1974, p. 37).

In my nonsexist practice I hope to encourage women to strike out and dare to be different—but I also must have empathy with those for whom the struggle is still too great. I must have an understanding of the

> pivotal position of this generation of young women who are living in a transitional phase of psychosocial evolution, struggling to consolidate a feminine identity from that of their predecessors, and developing personalities that will be the basis of identification for the next generation (Menaker, 1982, p. 83).

In a study of feminist concepts of therapy outcome, Kaschak (1976) noted that outcome is more likely to involve redefinition of a woman's self-image when her self-image is no longer anchored in the achievements and expectations of the men in her life. Women are often afraid of not feeling strong and in control—a kind of false pretense they have adopted as a defense against the weakness and incompetency society expects of them (Miller, 1976). When a woman no longer has to act primarily to please another, can satisfy her own desires, can begin to know herself, then the woman struggles for authenticity, which is really a continuous process of changing her vision of herself.

REFERENCES

American Psychological Association. Report of the task force on sex bias and sex-role stereotyping in psychotherapeutic practice. *American Psychologist,* 1975, *30,* 1169–1175.

Anchor, K. N., Strassberg, D. S., & Elkins, D. Supervisors' perceptions of the relationships between therapist self-disclosure and clinical effectiveness. *Journal of Clinical Psychology,* 1976, *32* (1), 158.

Bent, R. J., Putnam, D. G., Kiesler, D. J. & Nowicki, S. Correlates of successful and unsuccessful psychotherapy. *Journal of Consulting and Clinical Psychology,* 1976, *44* (1), 149.

Berger, M. M. The impact of the therapist's personality on group process. *American Journal of Psychoanalysis*, Fall, 1974, *34* (3), 213–219.

Brody, C. M. Therapist as group model, therapist as group participant: Overcoming the imposter phenomenon. American Psychological Association Division 29 Midwinter Meeting, Monterey, Calif., March 1981.

Bugental, J. F. T. *The search for authenticity*. New York: Holt, Rinehart & Winston, 1965.

Chesler, P. Women as psychiatric and psychotherapeutic patients. In R. K. Unger & F. L. Denmark, *Woman: Dependent or independent variable?* New York: Psychological Dimensions, 1975, pp. 137–162.

Condry, J., & Dyer, S. Fear of success: Attribution of cause to the victim. *Journal of Social Issues*, 1976, *32* (3), 85–98.

Darley, S. A. Big time careers for little women: A dual role dilemma. *Journal of Social Issues*, 1976, *32* (3), 85–98.

Delk, J. L., & Ryan, T. T. A-B status and sex-stereotyping among psychotherapists and patients. *Journal of Nervous and Mental Diseases*, April 1977, *164* (4), 253–262.

Friedman, G. The mother-daughter bond. *Contemporary Psychoanalysis*, January 1980, *16* (1), 90–97.

Hare-Mustin, R. T. A feminist approach to family therapy. *Family Processes*, June 1978, *17*, 181–194.

Hoffman, L. W. Early childhood experiences and women's achievement motives. *Journal of Social Issues*, 1972, *28* (2), 129–155.

Horner, M. S. Toward an understanding of achievement-related conflicts in women. *Journal of Social Issues*, 1972, *28*, (2), 157–175.

Johnson, M. An approach to feminist therapy. *Psychotherapy: Theory, Research and Practice*, Spring 1976, *13* (1), 72–76.

Kaschak, E. Sociotherapy: An ecological model for therapy with women. *Psychotherapy: Theory, Research and Practice*, Spring 1976, *13* (1), 61–63.

Kaslow, F., Cooper, B., & Linsenberg, M. Family therapist authenticity as a key factor in outcome. *International Journal of Family Therapy*, Summer 1979, *1* (2), 184–199.

Lessing, Doris. Preface to *The golden notebook*. In D. Lessing, *A small personal voice*. New York: Knopf, 1974, pp. 23–44.

LoPiccolo, J., & Herman, J. Cultural values and the therapeutic definition of sexual function and dysfunction. *Journal of Social Issues*, 1977, *33* (2), 166–183.

Menaker, E. The therapy of women in the light of psychoanalytic theory and the emergence of a new view. In V. Franks & V. Burtle (Eds.), *Women in therapy*. New York: Brunner/Mazel, 1974, pp. 230–246.

Menaker, E. Female identity in psychosocial perspective. *Psychoanalytic Review*, Spring 1982, *69* (1), 75–83.

Miller, J. B. *Towards a new psychology of women*. Boston: Beacon Press, 1976.

Mogul, K. M. The sex of the therapist. *American Journal of Psychiatry*, January 1982, *139* (1), 1–11.

Rawlings, E. I., & Carter, D. K. *Psychotherapy for women*. Springfield, Ill.: Charles C. Thomas, 1977.

Moulton, R. The role of Clara Thompson in the psychoanalytic study of women. In J. Strouse, *Women and analysis*. New York: Grossman, 1974.

Whitehorn, J., & Betz, B. Further studies of the doctor as a crucial variable in the outcome of treatment with schizophrenic patients. *American Journal of Psychiatry*, 1960, *117*, 215–223.

Williams, E. *Notes of a feminist therapist*. New York: Praeger, 1976.

■ 2

The Therapist as Imposter[1]

MARGARET S. GIBBS

In this paper I will discuss those aspects of the profession of psychotherapy that may predispose the practitioner to feelings of being an imposter. Further, I would like to suggest that imposter feelings among therapists may affect the teaching and practice of psychotherapy in directions that could be conceptualized as gender-stereotyped.

I discovered the label "imposter" years after identifying the feeling in myself. I never had the feeling Clance and Imes (1978) describe of being an intellectual imposter: I was brought up to believe myself intelligent by my family and my experiences at school were positive. Once I began my work as a therapist, however, I began to have imposter doubts. Certainly my supervisors seemed to approve of my work and my patients improved as much as anybody else's did. But what was I actually supposed to be *doing?* I knew the dynamic, client-centered, and behavioral theories, but I continued to read and search for answers. I felt there was something else I should know, something my instructors had neglected to tell me, much as cooks are said to withhold one important ingredient of their recipes when they relinquish them.

1. This chapter is based on a paper presented at a Symposium: Overcoming the impostor phenomenon, at the APA Division 29 Midwinter Meeting, February 1982.

My insecurity was at least partly due to lack of experience. I became more confident as I in fact became a better therapist through experience. Lurking doubts remained, however. They emerged when I had especially difficult cases; they emerged when I went for licensing exams and for the ABPP diplomate; and they emerged when I taught. The graduate course I taught in counseling and therapy was my favorite, but it also aroused the most anxiety. The more honest I was about what I did as a therapist, the more vulnerable and exposed I felt. Although students liked the course, I felt threatened when they echoed my own bewildered feelings as a student, "But what actually am I supposed to *do?*" If they thought *I* was holding back on the secret ingredient, they were mistaken.

A colleague showed me the Clance and Imes article about the impostor phenomenon at around the same time as I was finding its cure. I joined a group of peer supervision and was enormously surprised and reassured to find that all of its skilled and experienced members at times shared doubts equivalent to my own. I also shared experiences with others who were sitting or had sat for the ABPP exam and discovered that, to a man and a woman, all felt the same insecurity. As several persons expressed it, "I felt like I was finally going to be showed up for the fraud I was." My own feelings of fraudulence lessened as I recognized how general such feelings were, and I began to focus on the "fraudulence" of the profession.

THE PROFESSION OF PSYCHOTHERAPY AND IMPOSTER FEELINGS

I wondered what it could be about being a psychotherapist that could elicit such insecurity in persons at the demonstrated top of their profession (since all such "impostors" passed their ABPP exam). One of the most obvious difficulties with being a therapist is the ambiguity about how well one is actually doing. Computer programmers, for instance, often say that one of the joys of their profession is the immediate feedback of success when the job is correctly completed. No such joy awaits the therapist. First of all, since according to Bergin and Lambert (1978), the best estimate of spontaneous remission lies between 43 and 53 percent, and the average success rate of psychotherapy is still about two-thirds, then only about 20 percent of patients improve in therapy who otherwise would not have improved. Theoretically, then, only about one time in five can most therapists legitimately feel success. Second, a therapist has little way of determining an individual success rate in comparison to the overall success rate for the profession. The difficulties of outcome studies are well known, and carrying out any type of self-study that would generate meaningful outcome data on one's overall effectiveness is well-nigh impossible. Third, even when one manages to feel successful as a therapist, it is extremely difficult to pinpoint which of many interventions, interpretations, and aspects of the therapy situation led to the patient's improvement. In this connection, I am often reminded of a colleague who employed his entire repertoire of techniques to help a disturbed patient. He asked her after her recovery what had helped her and she replied, "It was the way you wiggle your foot. When you do that, I always know you care."

In short, the therapist lacks contingent reinforcement. In addition, cultural attitudes about therapy may affect the therapist's confidence. Expectations from patients range from the hope of the magic cure, which the therapist knows it is impossible to fill, to complete distrust and lack of understanding. I can recognize that some of my own self-doubts about being a clinician stem from my family's lack of understanding of psychotherapy as a profession. The pervasiveness of such attitudes may affect other clinicians even when their family and immediate associates are more enlightened.

It is interesting to note that almost every theory about psychotherapy has built into it a construct that functions to assuage impostor feelings on the part of its practitioners. Rogers in his early days stressed non-directiveness; it was up to the client, not the therapist, to find the answers and directions for change. Later, as it became clear that nondirectiveness was wishful thinking on the part of the therapist, that all of us were at least indirectly directive, Rogers stated that the necessary and sufficient conditions for therapeutic change were met if the therapist created the proper atmosphere of warmth, genuineness, and empathy. If the patient did not then improve, she or he did not perceive the atmosphere accurately, and there was nothing further the therapist could do. What a relief! The notion of resistance in the psychodynamic framework can also be viewed within such a functionalist perspective. While the therapist is responsible for helping the patient perceive and analyze the resistance, there is no guarantee whatsoever that it can be overcome. Whenever therapy does not succeed, the therapist can always fault the resistance. The gestalt notion of patient "respons-ability" can be seen as a similar loophole for the therapist; the aspects of many humanist theories that stress the patient's strengths and capabilities may actually be used to let the therapist off the hook in feeling responsibility for the outcome of therapy. London (1964) argued that behaviorism is a more moral mode of therapy since it requires the therapist to take responsibility for the outcome. In thinking about this difference between behavior therapy and other therapies, it appears to me that it is not that behaviorists are more moral, but that they have less need of a rationale to explain failure. That is, either they are more successful, or in some other way they are more sure of what they are doing. Since Smith and Glass (1977) have demonstrated that they are not, in fact, more successful, some other area of self-certainty must be available to them that is not available to other therapists.

One major area of difference has to do with the clarity of the goals and operations used by behaviorists as compared to other clinicians. Behaviorists need not live with the same amount of ambiguity as most therapists. The behaviorist knows what to *do*, can answer the query of the bewildered student, "What should I *do?*" I use an excellent paperback in my therapy course, *How to do psychotherapy and how to evaluate it*, by Gottman and Leiblum (1974). It is, of course, largely behavioral in orientation; what other point of view could represent itself with so much authority in 157 pages on so vast a topic? It always reminds me of books like *How to make electrical repairs*, or *How to install new flooring in your own home*. Needless to say, the students like the book, as I do myself. I have developed a tendency to rely on similar books in my course, books that focus on techniques and practical operations. I think this is desirable since students need a great deal of practical guidance in their beginning work as therapists. As I pondered the nature of the impostor phenomenon, however, I realized that the focus on the "how to" was partly because it relieved some of my own sense of insecurity about the ambiguity of my discipline. This aspect of the choice is not desirable; the ambiguity is inherent in at least parts of our discipline, I think. I began to wonder how many other instructors focused on the "how-to" to avoid impostor feelings.

INSTRUMENTAL VERSUS EXPRESSIVE ORIENTATION AS GENDER-TYPED

The focus on "doing" versus "being" and "feeling" can be conceptualized as instrumental versus expressive. Almost 30 years ago Parsons and Bales (1955) originated this dimension to define roles within the family and society. The instrumental orientation is a task orientation—a goal outlook that seeks efficient and effective answers to concrete problems. The expressive orientation is more emotional—an outlook that seeks to support the system in a more ambiguous and less concrete way through building morale and cohesion. The behavioral approach and other "how-to" approaches to therapy (rational-emotive, problem-solving, and so on) are instrumental; dynamic, client-centered, humanistic, and other less "problem-centered" approaches are much more expressive. These latter approaches seek to accomplish goals that are broader, harder to operationalize, and more directly related to interpersonal and emotional functioning (self-actualization, insight, awareness, character change, and so forth). Since behavioral goals are more defined, outcomes can be better assessed. Thus behaviorists have less of the ambiguity about effectiveness, as well as the ambiguity about what to do. In addition, the expectations and attitudes of the culture about receiving help are much more congruent with the concrete directives on self-improvement from the behavioristic orientation than they are with slow, indirectly guided self-exploration.

When Parsons and Bales developed the instrumental–expressive concept, their purpose was to explain gender roles within the family, women of course being expressive, males instrumental. While the concept might appear to be outdated, and is certainly stereotypical, recent research on male and female friendship patterns has convinced my colleagues and me (Fox, Gibbs, & Auerbach[2]) that the distinction is still viable and has explanatory force in accounting for gender differences. Applying the concept here means that the behavioral orientation is more stereotypically male, the dynamic-humanistic orientation more stereotypically female. Indeed, it is difficult to think of women who have made central contributions to behavior therapy, while renowned expressive female therapists come rapidly to mind—Virginia Axline, Helene Deutsch, Anna Freud, Frieda Fromm-Reichman, Melanie Klein, Virginia Satir, Jesse Taft, and Clara Thompson for a few prominent examples. This is certainly not to assert that there are no women in the forefront of behaviorism, but simply that they seem not to have made such a marked contribution as they have to more expressive modes of therapy.

Other important polarities within psychology could be conceptualized as male–female sex-typed. That is, therapy as an art versus therapy as a science can be viewed as an anima–animus dichotomy linked to the

---

2. Fox, M., Gibbs, M. S., & Auerbach, D. Gender and age dimensions of friendship. To be published in *Psychology of Women Quarterly*.

stereotyped skills and orientations of females (verbal, intuitive) and males (mathematical). Similarly, the practitioner–researcher dichotomy, as old as James' distinction between the tender-hearted and the tough-minded, is probably another female–male division. Rather than attempt to deal with these other very encompassing polarities, I am going to discuss only the expressive–instrumental distinction as it is gender-typed.

There is some empirical support for the idea that women are more expressive therapists than men, forming closer emotional bonds with their patients. Jones and Zoppel (1982) compared the ratings of 160 male and female therapists and 99 male and female clients chosen from a broad sample of outpatient settings. Female therapists perceived patients of both sexes, but particularly female patients, in more positive terms. Men, for instance, more frequently than women, applied the terms "simple, affected, commonplace, conventional, and tempermental" to their female patients, whereas women were more likely to apply the terms "capable, healthy, understanding, efficient, and intelligent" to their female patients. Women therapists achieved more consensus in their ratings of patients and, more than male therapists, rated their patients as improved on 5 of 11 rating scales.

The ratings of clients provided some support for the view of female therapists as to the effectiveness of their therapy. Thirty-eight interview items taken from Strupp, Wallach, and Wogan (1964) were administered to clients and factor analyzed. Female therapists were rated higher by their clients on the first factor, the therapeutic alliance, tapping therapist interest in, acceptance of, and respect for the client. This is congruent with the ratings of clients by therapists, indicating greater female respect for clients. A third factor, emotional intensity, was higher (at near significance level) for female therapists paired with female patients. This indicated that for this pairing, therapy was an emotional experience, sometimes associated with the expression of angry feelings toward the therapist or with exploration of childhood experiences. These two factors were the only ones to correlate positively and significantly with global outcome ratings. It should be noted that client global outcome ratings did not themselves significantly differentiate male and female therapists except in minor respects, although the authors express some doubts about the form and sensitivity of the five-item global rating scale.

The Jones and Zoppel (1982) findings can be viewed as indicating that women therapists are, on the average, superior to men therapists at the expressive aspects of therapy. Such a finding is compatible with our findings (Fox, Gibbs, & Auerbach[3]) as to the greater expressive element in women's friendships as compared to men's; one would expect therapeutic relationships to be similar in at least some respects to other types of relationships. One aspect of the expressive dimension, empathy, has been found by other writers to be gender-linked. Hoffman's 1977 review found that women exhibit more capacity for vicarious empathy, the capacity to experience the feeling of another, than do men. Lambert, DeJulio, and Stein (1978) suggest in their review of several studies, some using counselors, that women may be more sensitive in the judgment of feelings than men. The weight of the evidence, then, seems supportive of the idea that women are probably better able than men to perceive and use emotions effectively within a therapeutic alliance.

THE VALUE OF ANDROGENY IN THERAPY

What are the strengths of male therapists, then? If the differences between the effectiveness of male and female therapists are small (Jones & Zoppel, 1982), then males should have some compensating abilities. One possibility is the greater status of men in our society, lending them more power to use persuasion and suggestion with their clients. Goldstein and Simonson (1971), for instance, have suggested the importance of status within the therapy relationship. Another possibility may be greater instrumentality in men. Although there is no empirical evidence of greater instrumentality for male therapists, it seems likely to be the case. Male therapists may exert a powerful impetus to change by focusing on patient goals and using their status to create direct and subtle pressures for patients to meet these goals. It is my impression from years of teaching and supervising that many male graduate students react negatively to the Rogerian approach, because they are uncomfortable dealing with feelings but also because they need approaches that allow them to be more directive. Female graduate students generally have no such difficulties.

I believe that a balance of expressivity and instrumentality within psychotherapy is to be desired. (Such an integration appears to be occurring naturally, as behaviorism incorporates more cognitive and emotional

3. Fox, M., Gibbs, M. S., & Auerbach, D., op. cit.

elements and dynamic approaches become more short-term and goal oriented.) It appears to me that androgynous therapists are probably the most effective and that our training of therapists should take this into account.

There is one study that can be interpreted as supporting the value of androgyny in therapy. Bloom, Wiegel, and Trautt (1977) compared the reactions of college subjects who were asked to imagine themselves as the patients of either a male or a female therapist presented in either a "humanistic" or a "traditional" office. The humanistic office contained posters with sayings like "Today is the first day of the rest of your life," two identical chairs for patient and therapist placed less than a yard apart, and a bean bag chair in another corner. The traditional office contained diplomas in place of the posters, placed patient and therapist at either side of a desk, about five feet apart, and had a filing cabinet and professional texts. Otherwise the rooms were identical. Subjects rated the therapist whose office they had seen on aspects of credibility. Female therapists were rated as more dynamic and more generally credible in the traditional office than in the humanistic office. Male therapists were rated as safer and were more likely to be recommended to a friend when they were seen in the humanistic office. Bloom, Weigel, and Trautt interpret their data by saying that incongruent communications are perceived as more credible, i.e., that women and men are seen as more credible in situations that are not stereotypically associated with their gender. A simpler and more logical explanation is that when choosing a therapist, an individual wants an androgynous person, one who can be both expressive and instrumental. The offices gave cues that reassured subjects that the male therapists in the humanistic offices could be "soft" and the female therapists in the traditional offices could be professional.

Clinical psychology seems to me a fine place to promote androgyny, partly because therapists so often become models, and partly because androgyny already exists within it to a large extent. In clinical psychology we have men who make a career of caring for others, who generally know how to deal on an expressive level with their patients. We also have women who have had to show high instrumentality in the pursuit of their doctoral degrees and careers. In spite of possible animus–anima distinctions between research and practice, male and female psychologists who recently received their doctorates are represented in roughly equal proportions across different occupational settings—academia, clinical practice, and research (Stapp & Fulcher, 1982).

Psychology as a profession has in fact been more supportive of women than most other professional disciplines. Emmons (1982) cites government figures indicating that 41 percent of all doctorates in psychology go to women, whereas the percentage of doctorates awarded to women overall is 29 percent. This acceptance of women may be related to the emphasis on the expressive dimension in psychology.

One thing that struck me originally when I was discovering the generality of the impostor phenomenon among clinicians I knew was that males seemed to share it equally with females. I certainly did not go about my survey in any scientific fashion, but male colleagues seemed to fear their own possible fraudulence as much as female colleagues. (Most of my colleagues are relatively dynamic and humanistic in their outlook; I cannot speak to the question of whether behaviorists experience the impostor phenomenon. The argument presented here would suggest that they do not to the same extent.)

Clance and Imes (1978) described the impostor phenomenon as an experience primarily felt by women, and primarily in relation to academic and intellectual success. (See Chapter 6 by Imes and Clance in this volume for a full discussion.) I was interested to see that several female colleagues who had deep and unwarranted impostor feelings about their professional and intellectual competence reported they had always felt exceedingly comfortable and effective in their roles as therapists, untroubled by the ambiguity that bothered me. Clance's recent research has indicated that impostor feelings are more acute the more the woman's role has not been accepted by her family, ethnic group, and culture. It may well be that women are less prone to impostor feelings in the stereotypically female, expressive therapist role. Since such a role is contrary to male stereotypes, men may be more prone to the experience than in many other occupational roles.

THE PRESSURES FOR INSTRUMENTALITY

I think, though, that in spite of the recognition of the importance of expressivity in a good therapist, there are pressures, at least within the academic setting that I know best, toward instrumentality. For instance, in spite of the spate of supportive evidence from Fiedler (1950) to Gurman (1977), the Rogerian relationship approach to psychotherapy has never achieved the status, at least within academic circles, accorded to behaviorism. In spite of much evidence for the comparability in effectiveness of behavioral to other approaches when they are carefully controlled (Sloan, Staples, Cristol, Yorkston, & Whipple, 1975; Smith, Glass, & Miller, 1980), behaviorism remains more academically respectable, probably because of its stress on operationalism and its ties to laboratory research, i.e., its greater instrumentality. It may be that instrumentality is favored because it is the more masculine approach. It may be that it is favored because it, as we have discussed, may assuage impostor feelings. It may be that it reduces impostor feelings because it is the more masculine approach. At any rate, I do feel that within academia, where all our therapists are taught, there is a notion that "real" psychology is experimental, operational, and instrumental.

Pressure toward instrumentality involves some role conflict for women since it also means pressure to move out of the stereotypically feminine role into a "masculine" role which will be perceived negatively. As a male psychologist in my department put it after listening to a female behaviorist speak about her research and therapy, "It just goes to prove that any woman who does that kind of work has to be cold." In spite of the likelihood of increased impostor feelings as women move into instrumental fields, women, like all therapists, should be encouraged to incorporate as much goal-oriented technique as is feasible within their clinical procedures.

For men, the pressures toward instrumentality often show themselves in an outward denial of the expressive capacity that appears in their actual work with patients. I have known several male clinicians who described themselves as hard-nosed, manipulative problem-solvers as therapists, self-descriptions which apparently defended against impostor feelings, since their patients usually described them as pussycats. Male psychologists, like all men, need more support and reinforcement for their expressive side. Instructors in psychology could attempt to provide such support more explicitly than they usually do.

In our training of psychotherapists, I think it is helpful to keep in mind the need to integrate expressive and instrumental approaches and to keep in mind the pressures toward instrumentality. Expressive concepts like "being with" the patient, the "I and thou," "here and now feelings," "authenticity," "therapeutic love," "listening with the third ear," and "accurate empathy" are impossible to fully operationalize, hard to teach in any fashion, and easy to ridicule. Nevertheless, I think that the expressive dimension is essential to good therapy and that it is a mistake to ignore it because it is imprecise. Training in psychotherapy should be training for the whole person, the anima as well as the animus.

Even training in expressive therapy can become overly instrumental when the focus becomes specific techniques and procedures alone. The pressure toward instrumentality includes as well the pressure to produce the one "right answer" to any potential patient problem. Such strategies can cover up, but not resolve, the ambiguities of clinical judgments and interventions. Impostor doubts need to be shared, not suppressed, in the classroom as elsewhere. Arkes (1981) cites evidence to support the idea that uncertainty and humility about the accuracy of our clinical inferences is an aid to increased accuracy. I find this notion enormously comforting.

REFERENCES

Arkes, H. Impediments to accurate clinical judgment and possible ways to mini-mize their impact. *Journal of Consulting and Clinical Psychology*, 1981, *49*, 323–330.

Bergin, A. E., & Lambert, M. J. The evaluation of therapeutic outcomes. In S. L. Garfield & A. E. Bergin (Eds.), *Handbook of psychotherapy and behavior change: An empirical analysis* (2nd ed.). New York: Wiley, 1978.

Bloom, L. J., Weigel, R. G., & Trautt, G. M. "Therapeugenic" factors in psychotherapy: Effects of office decor and subject–therapist sex pairing on the perception of credibility. *Journal of Consulting and Clinical Psychology*, 1977, *45*, 867–873.

Clance, P. R., & Imes, S. The impostor phenomenon in high achieving women: Dynamics and therapeutic intervention. *Psychotherapy: Theory, Research and Practice*, 1978, *15*, 241–247.

Emmons, C. A longitudinal study of the careers of a cohort of assistant professors in psychology. *American Psychologist*, 1982, *37*, 1228–1238.

Fiedler, F. E. The concept of an ideal therapeutic relationship. *Journal of Consulting Psychology*, 1950, *14*, 239–245.

Goldstein, A. P., & Simonson, N. R. Social psychological approaches to psychotherapy research. In A. E. Bergin & S. L. Garfield (Eds.), *Handbook of psychotherapy and behavior change: An empirical analysis*. New York: Wiley, 1971.

Gottman, J. M., & Leiblum, S. R. *How to do psychotherapy and how to evaluate it: A manual for beginners*. New York: Holt, Rinehart & Winston, 1974.

Gurman, A. S. The patient's perception of the therapeutic relationship. In A. S.

Gurman & A. M. Razin (Eds.), *Effective psychotherapy: A handbook of research*. Oxford: Pergamon, 1977.

Hoffman, M. L. Sex differences in empathy and related behaviors. *Psychological Bulletin*, 1977, *84*, 712–722.

Jones, E., & Zoppel, C. Client and therapist gender and psychotherapy. *Journal of Consulting and Clinical Psychology*, 1982, *50*, 259–272.

Lambert, M. J., DeJulio, S. S., & Stein, D. M. Therapist interpersonal skills: Process, outcome, methodological considerations, and recommendations for future research. *Psychological Bulletin*, 1978, *85*, 467–488.

London, P. *The modes and morals of psychotherapy*. New York: Holt, Rinehart & Winston, 1964.

Parsons, T., & Bales, R. F. *Family socialization and interaction process*. Glencoe, Ill.: The Free Press, 1955.

Sloan, R. B., Staples, F. R., Cristol, A. H., Yorkston, N. J., & Whipple, K. *Psychotherapy versus behavior therapy*. Cambridge, Mass.: Harvard University Press, 1975.

Smith, M. L., & Glass, G. V. Meta-analysis of psychotherapy outcome studies. *American Psychologist*, 1977, *32*, 752–760.

Smith, M. L., Glass, G. V., & Miller, T. I. *The benefits of psychotherapy*. Baltimore: Johns Hopkins University Press, 1980.

Stapp, J., & Fulcher, R. The employment of 1979 and 1980 doctorate recipients in psychology. *American Psychologist*, 1982, *37*, 1159–1185.

Strupp, H. H., Wallach, M. S., & Wogan, M. Psychotherapy experience in retrospect: Questionnaire survey of former patients and their therapists. *Psychological Monographs*, 1964, *78* (11, Whole No. 588).

■ two

FEMINISM AND PSYCHOANALYSIS

■3

The Convergence of Psychoanalysis and Feminism: Gender Identity and Autonomy

JESSICA BENJAMIN

THE EVOLUTION OF FEMINIST THINKING IN PSYCHOANALYSIS

The contemporary upsurge of feminism brought with it a wave of rejection, revolt, and criticism directed at psychoanalysis. This initial repudiation was provoked by the psychoanalytic acceptance of women's derogated status in patriarchal culture. Obvious targets of feminist critique were Freud's view of women as penisless, morally undeveloped creatures and the misuse of psychoanalysis as an adjustment therapy designed to reconcile unhappy women to the feminine mystique. But rather quickly feminists also recognized a few early analytic foremothers, such as Karen Horney, who challenged Freud's positions on femininity. Against this backdrop, Juliet Mitchell (1974) was the first to argue for the reappropriation of psychoanalysis by feminists as a theory of patriarchy in which the penis as a symbol does play a central role. She contended that the unconscious content of our mental lives is shaped by patriarchal relations. In America Mitchell's arguments evoked more esteem than resonance, largely because of their abstractness.

The impact of American psychoanalytic feminists, on the other hand, has been far more profound. Nancy Chodorow (1978) and Dorothy Dinnerstein (1976) offered to feminists a psychoanalytic perspective which emphasized not the primacy of the phallus but the significance of women's mothering. Their work corresponded to a crucial shift in mainstream psychoanalytic thought, from a focus on the Oedipus complex to the pre-oedipal issues of separation–individuation in the mother–child relationship. Freud's neglect of the mother in favor of the oedipal father was now reversed as the issue of early separation pushed sexuality out of the spotlight. In particular, Chodorow's analysis of how female gender identity—especially its positive aspects—develops in response to female mothering was too pertinent for even antipsychoanalytic feminists to ignore. The focus on women's mothering suggested that psychoanalysis had more to offer than a theory of penis envy. The early interplay of gender identity formation, self-formation, and the persistence of issues related to these processes in adult life could now be investigated in a new way.

The initial lack of psychoanalytic attention to mothering corresponds to what Freud recognized as a central component of the masculine psyche, "the repudiation of femininity" (Freud, 1937). His own theory of the Oedipus complex is a vital contribution to the understanding of that repudiation, although he attributed it to the bedrock of nature rather than to patriarchal culture. Even if unalterable natural facts of anatomy play a role in the origins of patriarchy, it is quite another matter to use these facts to justify the continuation of male domination in an advanced technological world. The argument against Freud is that we and our theories are socially constructed, and our conscious intentions play a role in the constructing. On the other hand, it is not only our conscious intentions that determine what we do. Equally important in understanding the depth and persistence of patriarchy is access to the unconscious. With these reservations in mind, feminist intentions and psychoanalytic explanations may approach one another more closely.

Freud's theory of development, especially his theory of the Oedipus complex, shows how boys come to be men by repudiating their primary identification with their mothers (Freud, 1923, 1924). It is a theory about the repudiation of femininity. At the same time it is a model of how individuality develops in our culture since male development is seen as standard and female development as a deviation. In the sense that it describes a socially normative or real phenomenon, it is not an inaccurate theory. Rather, it is one-sided, the light side of a globe whose full meaning becomes apparent only when seen together with the dark side as part of a whole. The theory of the Oedipus complex explains why this ideal of individuality has been so one-sided by showing its roots in the identification with paternal authority and the repudiation of maternal nurturance. The crux of our cultural ideal of autonomy is that it stands for radical opposition to mutuality, dependency, connectedness, and nurturance. By focusing not on women's lack of a penis but on male repudiation of mothering, feminism could throw into question a model of individuality in which autonomy and self-assertion are considered more important than empathy, nurturance, and caring for others. To understand the unconscious roots of this ideal, however, to free ourselves from the deep-seated antagonism between the impulses for self-assertion and relatedness, requires a *psychoanalytic* feminism. It requires an investigation of early identifications and experiences with the mother, and her counterpart, the father.

In the Oedipus complex, as Freud first articulated it, the crucial step in self-development comes through the enactment of a drama in the triangle. The male child loves his mother and wishes to possess her, hates his father and wishes to replace/murder him. In return, the child fears the power of the father, his ability to take from him that which makes him male and separates him from mother—the penis. In a successful resolution of the complex, the boy internalizes the paternal authority and renounces his love for the mother (Freud, 1923). In exchange, he hopes to become like his father and to possess someone like mother after all. The compensation for his loss of the mother as love-object is the success in maintaining the father as "like-object," the person with whom he identifies. In renouncing his sexual wish toward the mother, the boy is actually renouncing his infancy love, which included his dependency, his vulnerability and clinging, his admiration of her power, his identification with her, and her nurturance. The Oedipus complex does not merely mean the renunciation of incest because of the castration threat. It also means the renunciation of the maternal world, and the repudiation of all that is associated with it.

From our point of view, the most important point in the idea of normal oedipal development is that the boy represses his identification with his mother, with things feminine. Heretofore the most important person to him, his model of what a grown-up person is, mother, is now replaced by father. The one object now becomes split into two, the object of love and the object of identification. Autonomy now means identification with the father. And the nature of the identification with the father is different from that with the mother—more distant, less personal, more competitive (Chodorow, 1978). The nature of the autonomy is: if I am strong like father I do not need her; if I am not like her, I can be independent like him. The power of the oedipal paradigm was to incorporate this experience by showing how gender identity and individual selfhood develop through intensely affective and sensual bonds that only young children and lovers know. At the same time, by incorporating essentially the masculine experience of development, including the renunciation of those early bonds, it equated masculinity with all individuality. The Oedipal father as the model for autonomy reverberates with the universal belief in our culture that the father represents the way into the world.

THE OEDIPUS COMPLEX AS A SEXUAL DIVISION OF LABOR

But to identify with this father and this model of autonomy is also to accept the irreconcilability of two essential human needs, those for connectedness and for individuality. It is to see nurturance as the price of freedom. This is the cultural and personal polarity which is institutionalized in the Oedipus complex, and which is given the form of gender. It is apparent, then, that the Oedipus complex is the psychological embodiment of the sexual division of labor. The theory offers an explanation of how the deepest human needs become constructed in such a way that people accept this division of labor (Benjamin, 1981). It also explains, although unwittingly, the fact that these gender positions are so irreconcilable—you may identify with only one parent, may only be like either mother or father. Hence you may be only dependent or independent, nurturant or self-contained, subject or object. The problem which this analysis of the Oedipus complex reveals is the polarizing of our needs for freedom and nurturance, of our capacities for relatedness and self-assertion. This polarity of needs corresponds to the predominant gender ideals as either active male hyperindividuation or passive female renunciation of individuality.

Before we pursue the implications of this view of gender for women, which my schematic presentation of the male version of development leaves out, let us consider a different ideal of individuality. Let us suppose the existence of these original dualities in human capacities: connection and separation; difference and likeness; desire for the new and the wish to return to the familiar. These opposites form a creative tension within the individual. This tension is, of course, the real core of the study of early separation–individuation, of the growth of self within the parent–child dyad (Mahler, Pine, & Bergman, 1975). And as long as the child's self is conceptualized in terms of the dyad, the need for both sides of the polarity is usually recognized. The young child's need is indeed to find recognition for both self-assertion and relatedness, separateness and closeness. For that matter, as feminists have long argued, it is the mother's need, too, to be both connected to and separate from her child. Above all, this dual need of the mother has gone unrecognized by psychoanalysis.

GENDER IDENTITY AND AUTONOMY

It is this nonrecognition of the mother in theory which points to the problem in reality: that the child must not only become separate from the mother, but at some point be able to recognize that the mother herself is also a separate subject. That is, the child must recognize this because it sees the mother acting as an independent subject, just as it sees (by all accounts) its father acting. Practically, for the mother to embody the same kind of autonomous, active selfhood as the father implies monumental changes in society. Theoretically, it merely requires that we think about human development in the context of a relationship involving two subjects. We need to envision both mother and child as separate individuals, both connected to each other but also different people with different needs. This vision is a crucial part of curing the split between nurturance and freedom, and the split between the two genders. If the individual is to maintain a tension between two different needs, then she or he would have to be raised by someone who can maintain this tension within herself.

To some extent psychoanalytic theory has moved toward realizing these points by focusing on the early issues of separation–individuation in which separateness and oneness are so intertwined. And this theoretical shift has been accompanied by the tendency to acknowledge that psychoanalysis itself is a process involving two subjects in which not only interpretation but the relationship itself leads to change. On the other hand, the oedipal model casts its shadow over these early issues, both in the theory and in the reality. In the oedipal model, the polarity of needs is already a fact, inextricably part of gender identity as we know it. In psychoanalytic studies of early gender development, which now focus on the period of achieving core gender identity in the second half of the second year, the roles which mother and father play are already highly differentiated. The distinction between mother as love object and father as identification object are already seen as crucial to the little boy's establishment of masculine identity. The father is already important in helping the boy to identify his active desire for the mother and his desire to enter the world outside the mother—both ways to establish him*self* (Abelin, 1980). For the boy, the early recognition of gender difference is an advantage in the effort to differentiate his individuality from hers. As Chodorow (1978) has stressed, boys emerge from the pre-oedipal experience already emphasizing difference and distance, whereas girls continue to feel the continuity in relationship and identification with their mothers.

The feminist critique of the oedipal model (Chodorow, 1978; Gilligan, 1982) has made clear that women, in retaining their capacity for nurturance and empathy, embody that valuable side of human potential which men have renounced and devalued. This critique is decisive, for it throws into question the patriarchal assumptions about human nature that have been developed in Western thought and absorbed by psychoanalysis. But it must also be added that women continue to represent only one side of their own human capacities, albeit a side which deserves to be rescued from its current derogation. That is, we must consider the effect of the one-sided development on both genders. Girls may be equally unprepared to cope with separateness, although in a different way than boys. Their difficulty in perceiving mother as an independent subject ultimately makes them feel as lacking in subjectivity as she is. Their identification with her makes it more difficult for them to separate from her. During the rapprochement phase of separation–individuation, the child faces the anxiety of separation in the context of her or his efforts to become independent. In rapprochement the child realizes that in asserting itself and separating, it could lose the mother or clash with her independent subjectivity. Boys compensate for this loss by hurling themselves more into their motor activities. The bond with their fathers as well as their "greater motor-mindedness" makes them less likely than girls to be depressed in this phase (Mahler et al., 1975). The crisis of realizing their aloneness in the world, that mother is outside their control, is thus less acute.

What do little girls do with these same realizations, with this same dilemma of separation? If this problem is not naively ignored by psychoanalysis, it is suggested that girls may also identify with their fathers. But this identification is not part of a "natural" process of gender identity formation; rather, it always includes knowledge of difference. If this knowledge is not so painful that it is utterly denied, then it becomes a source of conflict. The girl-child has every reason to wish for a reconciliation between her contradictory strivings for oneness and separateness. The little girl's identification with her mother is strengthened as she becomes aware of gender, but so is her ambivalence. For she, too, must perceive the father as the source of freedom, the model of autonomy. If she prefers her femininity, the way is paved for her to displace some of her desire for activity into nurturing others, her sexual activity into pleasing her father's heroic successors. This is the solution to the problem of autonomy which so consistently fails for women: the fall back into object status, to being the supporter, nurturer, or pleaser. At the same time she is constantly measuring herself against an ideal of autonomy which expressly excludes nurturing and pleasing. As a little girl, she asks herself how she can *be* feminine like mother and yet *become* like father, separate and active. To some degree, the sense that she is aiming to become "like a man" haunts the enterprise of becoming a separate individual. The disparity between the ideal of autonomy and the ideal of femininity is a concrete dilemma of early girlhood, one which persists consciously and unconsciously into adult life.

WORKING ON THE ISSUE OF AUTONOMY

We now see that what appeared as an ideological problem, a bias in the theory of psychoanalysis, actually reflects a real problem. While all human beings are born with the capacities for self-assertion and relatedness, in actual life these human possibilities come into conflict. And this conflict is structured by our gender system. The problem I have identified is that the predominant ideal, theory, and practice of autonomy in our culture is associated with the repudiation of the maternal and feminine. Practically, this means that women are struggling to incorporate an ideal of autonomy which is alien to them at its very core. Theoretically, it means that feminists are struggling to heal a split between autonomy and nurturance which reaches into the deepest layers of our culture and our psyche. Clinically, the implications of this problem are far too myriad to discuss in such a brief paper. But I would like to suggest a few ways in which this ideal of autonomy and women's struggle to develop the active, independent side of their nature affects the process of psychotherapy. These propositions all pertain to what I see as women's deep feeling that their femininity, their dependency, and their identification with their mother is hopelessly at odds with their autonomy and activity.

One manifestation of this hopelessness may be the mistrust of theory and theorizing which has been prevalent in the feminist movement. This has several components: first, the mistrust of theorizing as a masculine activity which deals in abstraction rather than concrete experience or feeling. This mistrust is understandable, but it also reflects a one-sided attitude, acceptance of the irreconcilability of intellectual and emotional activity, of idea and experience. This attitude has made for a reluctance to appropriate psychoanalysis in a critical spirit. Yet another motive for the rejection of psychoanalysis has been suggested by Mitchell (1974), who attributes feminist animosity toward psychoanalysis to a rejection of the idea of the unconscious. The emphasis on unconscious intrapsychic factors has the implication that we, as conscious subjects, do not determine our lives. Nor does it place the blame squarely on the present oppressive reality. The exaltation of intrapsychic reality and past over present external reality have been particularly unattractive to feminist therapists. It seems to "blame the victim" by stressing the complicity of our desires in our lack of autonomy. Finally, the early feelings of dependency on mother may surface in the psychoanalytic situation—in the transference—and momentarily threaten the felt autonomy of both participants. The therapist, too, may then have to confront her feelings about another person depending upon her or separating from her.

I have been arguing that early experience and development, which persist as unconscious, intrapsychic factors, do play a part in women's struggle for autonomy. In my view the therapist's role is not to share in the hopelessness about this early experience but to make it possible for women to tolerate the painful early feelings about their femininity, their separateness, and their dependency. The analytic situation can help us to see the unconscious images which express such feelings not simply as alien, distorted, and shameful but as a form of creative activity and self-expression. The point is neither to ward off nor gratify early dependency needs, but to analyze them in terms of the early issues of identification with and separation from mother and father. I believe the danger of focusing on the patient's present, positive efforts to achieve autonomy is that the adult is defending against the little girl's helplessness and bafflement about achieving her separate identity. The actual feeling of hopelessness often goes back to her felt inability to be like her father or leave her mother without being like him.

The therapeutic relationship tends to re-evoke the highly charged regressive feelings of dependency on mother. Without an adequate analysis of transference, the woman in therapy may either have to suppress her wish for separateness from her therapist (mother) or achieve it in gesture only by leaving precipitously. Since the strivings for separateness would in either case tend to rupture the relationship, the therapist is also drawn to repair the rupture by offering more support or focusing on the patient's other relationships. To work out the negative, separating, rejecting feelings toward the mother—along with the early rage, guilt, and fear— presupposes the acknowledgment of feelings of dependency within the therapeutic relationship. That is, it requires the acknowledgment of both participants that the person seeking help is not already living up to her ideal of autonomy. Such acknowledgment can only come sincerely with the help of therapists who believe that the struggle to reconcile dependency and autonomy is not hopeless. It is we who must be aware of the complexity of this tension without being daunted by it.

REFERENCES

Abelin, E. L. Triangulation, the role of the father and core gender identity during the rapprochement subphase. In R. R. Lax, S. Bach, & J. A. Burland (Eds.), *Rapprochement*. New York: Jason Aronson, 1980, pp. 151–170.

Benjamin, J. The oedipal riddle: Authority, autonomy and the new narcissism. In J. Diggins & M. Kann (Eds.), *The problem of authority in America*. Philadelphia: Temple University Press, 1981, pp. 195–224.

Chodorow, N. *The reproduction of mothering*. Berkeley: University of California Press, 1978.

Dinnerstein, D. *The mermaid and the minotaur*. New York: Harper & Row, 1976.

Freud, S. *The ego and the id* (1923). Standard Edition. London: Hogarth Press, 1961.

Freud, S. *The dissolution of the Oedipus complex* (1924). Standard Edition. London: Hogarth Press, 1961, pp. 173–179.

Freud, S. *Analysis terminable and interminable* (1937). Standard Edition. London: Hogarth Press, 1964, pp. 209–253.

Gilligan, C. *In a different voice*. Cambridge and London: Harvard University Press, 1982.

Mahler, M., Pine, F., & Bergman, A. *The psychological birth of the human infant*. New York: Basic Books, 1975.

Mitchell, J. *Psychoanalysis and feminism*. New York: Pantheon, 1974.

■4
Feminist Psychoanalysis: Theory and Practice

LUISE EICHENBAUM AND SUSIE ORBACH

Since its inception, psychoanalysis has been concerned with two sorts of questions. The first is how we come to be who we are-i.e. the dynamics of the construction of personality. The second is the implications this has for the clinical practice of psychoanalysis. In posing these questions, Freud and those who have followed him have grappled with the relationship between culture and personality, between the meaning of human nature and the possibilities that exist within the therapeutic relationship. In the last 15 years there has begun to emerge a feminist inquiry into the nature of women's psychology (Baker, 1976; Chodorow, 1978; Mitchell, 1975) and the development of a feminist therapy (Eichenbaum & Orbach, 1983a). In this chapter we will address how feminist concerns reshape the terrain on which psychological inquiry is based, i.e., we will try to show what issues we think are important in a consideration of women's psychology and how these shape the therapeutic relationship.

It goes without saying that all therapies are informed by a political perspective of one sort or another however vehemently the defenders of one particular school may suggest that their work is objective and value free. Considerations of how one sees, understands, interprets, and reinterprets, how one measures change, therapeutic success, and so on, exist within a framework that makes sense in reference to the perspective of the school of thought.

A starting point for our feminist psychoanalysis is the understanding that in this culture (and indeed all others known to anthropologists) girls and women have occupied a circumscribed place. This place has been one of second-class citizenship and girls' psychologies embody this understanding of their position in some fundamental ways. In other words, from our perspective, gender (Belotti, 1975; Money & Erhardt, 1972) is a central feature of psychological development that exists in the conscious minds of parents before the birth of a child and all those who interact with an infant from birth onward.

Gender as a category has entered psychoanalytic literature only recently (Stoller, 1969). The Freudian view assumes a kind of pregendered personality until the Oedipal period, when girls and boys learn their place in relation to parental identification. Juliet Mitchell (1975) extends Freud's approach and proposes an understanding of the acceptance of an inferiorized psychology of femininity through the girl's realization that she does not have the power to hold the mother, that the loss of the mother is a consequence of gender weakness. Drawing on the work of those in gender identity, Belotti (1975), Chodorow (1978), and Eichenbaum and Orbach (1983a) see the centrality of gender in a patriarchal society in the construction of personality from its inception (and preconception).

As clinicians and as women ourselves we see continual evidence of both the acceptance and the rebellion against women's subordination in our own and the psychologies of our clients and of the clients of those we supervise.

Psychoanalytic theory emerges out of the practice of a therapy in which the manifest and latent content of the analysands' conscious and unconscious desires, distress, and so on come up for examination. Within modern psychoanalysis (Balint, 1969; Guntrip, 1968; Winnicott, 1965) there has been a stress on theorizing the adult's psychology from the goings on within the therapy relationship, not so much as a transferential phenomenon per se in which the therapy relationship is a refraction of the oedipal relations, but as a reflection of the internal object relations of the person as they have developed over time. In other words, there has been a shift in the notion of individuals being libidinally arrested to a view in which "We do not so much grow out of our childhood, as grow over the top of it . . ." (Guntrip, 1970). This has special relevance when we think in terms of gender (or class and race for that matter) as the societal attitudes continually reinforce the space an individual may take up. One is not simply gendered at birth and not after; the socialization process for which we are parentally prepared is itself a gendered one. The theory that we propose draws heavily on our therapeutic practice in which an examination of the therapy relationship yields particular understandings in relation to women's psychology. This chapter is thus organized as follows: first we discuss a clinically derived theory and then we illustrate the therapy process.

THEORY FOR A FEMINIST THERAPY

The construction of femininity, the making of a woman, involves complex and painful processes in which mothers have responsibility for the psychological reproduction of their infants into the gendered categories of their particular social world. In the case of the mother–daughter relationship, this means that mothers, themselves second-class citizens, introduce and direct their daughters into a version of the same kind of life that they have led. This is not to say that mothers cannot hope for more for their daughters than they had for themselves, this is not to say that mothers don't try to give what they felt they didn't get, and this is not to say that mothers turn their daughters into carbon copies of themselves. It is to state rather that the mother, in preparing her daughter for a life within patriarchy, conveys to her consciously and unconsciously the parameters of experience, the emotional and material possibilities that exist in the world for women.

The process toward femininity starts at birth. The infant enters a social world which she must assimilate in the process of psychological development. In the early months of life, the infant is assumed to be merged with mother (Klein, 1975; Mahler, Pine, & Bergman, 1975; Spitz, 1965; Winnicott, 1958). Its sense of itself as a separate person is as yet undeveloped. There are a myriad of experiences that turn infants into human beings. Babies learn to eat, to soothe themselves or to be soothed, to see (Balikov, 1960), to speak, to crawl, and to walk. While the infant is not passive or a *tabula rasa* on which imprinting occurs, nevertheless such socializing experiences are not only mediated by the caregiver, they are highly influenced by her ideas, actions, and attitudes. In other words, developmental tasks occur in a relational context, one moreover in which most likely it is mother who provides the constant adult experience. In order for successful socialization to occur, girl infants need to acquire a feminine personality just as boys need to acquire a masculine one. Mothers are vested with transmitting social practices which are fundamentally unequal and hence problematic. Women who are themselves the recipients of the same problematic social laws arrive at motherhood with the job of teaching their daughters to be outwardly directed, to supress their own needs for nurturance, and to seek satisfaction and fulfillment in caring for others and enabling others to potentiate.

In the period of early dependency when baby and mother form, as it were, one psychological unit, mother's perception of the infant's needs directs her actions. Winnicot (1965, p. 85) suggests that mothers turn inward to create an empathetic bond:

> By and large mothers do in one way or another identify themselves with the baby that is growing within them, and in this way they achieve a very powerful sense of what the baby needs. . . . The mother through identification of herself with her infant knows what the baby feels like . . ."

Through the process of projective identification, then, mothers respond to the needs of their infants. But precisely because gender is such a central feature of personality development, this projective identification is shaped by mother's own experiences regarding nurturance. It is our conclusion that neither adulthood for women nor the mother's own early childhood has given her a continued experience of being consistently attended to and nurtured. Thus for a mother, being responsive to her infant's needs is rarely a straightforward process. The daughter's needs for contact, and the concomitant need for separation and autonomy, prove difficult for the mother. If her own needs are insufficiently met, it means that her personality embodies a taboo against following her own initiatives, against being psychologically separated, and there is a denial of her needs for emotional nurturance. She was brought up to expect neither nurturance nor autonomy. Her own psychology and sense of herself is permeated by the painful knowledge that a part of her—which we call the little-girl—is hidden away hungry and fearful. This repressed little-girl aspect of mother motivates and directs many of mother's ambivalent responses and initiations toward a daughter. It creates a tension in mother so that she is inconsistent in her relating. There is a push-pull dynamic in the mother–daughter relationship. Mother is inconsistent in relating to her daughter's needs in that sometimes she is emotionally available and accepting and at other times she appears harsh and unenabling. The results of a mother's ambivalence in responding to her daughter's needs in early infancy is that she communicates a message that the daughter cannot fully rely on mother, the first person she loves and depends on. The tensions the mother feels internally about needs are communicated in the nurturing process. Aware of a woman's lot, the mother unconsciously restrains and limits her daughter's future expectations for emotional nurturance. The daughter, responding to this tension and unable to control mother's actions, is confused and anxious. She creates an explanation for these experiences of psychological abandonment. A notion develops in which the daughter comes to feel that there must be something wrong with her needs, something amiss with her very self, if she generates such unpredictable responses. Insufficiently nurtured and rejected, the daughter is already absorbing critical lessons in femininity. She is taking in the idea that (1) she shouldn't expect too much, (2) life is inconsistent and requires a kind of continual shifting, and (3) there is something wrong with who she is.

The negative aspects of this early period spur her on to seek what she needs elsewhere. Paradoxically, while mother is unable to unambiguously respond during the time of her daughter's most obvious dependency, she may be unable to let go of her as the daughter seeks nurturance, experience, contact, and validation elsewhere. In other words, in the period that is thought of as separation–individuation, mother now may act as ambivalently toward the daughter's needs for separation as she does toward her needs for contact. The privation that mother suffers which makes her unable to furnish consistent nurturance now prevents her from letting her daughter separate in a supported way. She draws her daughter close and frequently and unwittingly interrupts her adventures and exploration of her separateness. She feels her daughter's moves toward psychological separation as a loss. Mother herself has an unseparated psychology and she looks for completion in her partner and in her child. Her need for psychological attachment and nurturance may lead her to keep her daughter close and to teach her to attend to mother's unmet needs. The cycle turns. The daughter, needy herself, stays attached to a needy mother toward whom she gives. She takes in and accustoms herself early on with an emotional law of patriarchal social relations. *She gives to another what she so needs herself.*

The girl's psychology develops with a fear and repression of her own needs and desires. These unmet needs are consciously and unconsciously rejected by the girl, who comes to understand them, and consequently a part of herself, as bad. An illegitimacy, a sense of undeserving and unentitlement, follows. The girl's psychology embodies feelings of unworthiness and self-hate.

In adult women who seek therapy (and, indeed, in those who may not), we see the results of early psychological development shaped by this kind of privation. Adult women frequently feel insecure in themselves, afraid of their feelings, critical of their needs, "empty inside," or filled with ideas of unworthiness and self-hatred. The woman's psychological boundaries are shaky, and frequently her internal sense of self is unclear; she seeks self-definition in relation to others.

A woman seeks therapy out of pain, confusion, anxiety, or distress which she feels unable to cope with on her own. The very search for therapy is a statement of the need she has for contact with another person. The contact she is seeking is, if you like, the missing nurturance, i.e., the unambivalent emotional understanding that mother was unable to provide her or indicate would be available to her.

THE PROCESS OF FEMINIST THERAPY

The developmental picture we have presented so far has very clear translation in the therapy process itself. The therapist hears about her client's feelings about herself, her needs, her anxieties, and so on within the developmental framework which informs our diagnostic picture. In our practice this developmental framework in turn governs the process of the therapy relationship and the "treatment" itself. In addition precisely because contact—unambivalent and consistent—has been missing from women's experience, contact is a critical feature of the therapy. In this respect the process of a feminist psychoanalytically oriented psychotherapy may appear to share similarities to a Winnicottian or Guntripian analysis. That is to say, there is a stress on acknowledging the meaning and the realness of the actual relationship as well as the connection between client and therapist, and many interpretations refer to this relationship. In addition, there is an understanding of a hidden part of the personality which so needs this contact and nurturance. Our hidden little-girl structurally conforms to Winnicott's (1965) "true self" and Fairbairn's (1952) and Guntrip's (1968) schizoid split.

In a feminist psychoanalysis, the therapist and client together follow the winding paths of the client's internal object relations and, traversing these paths, change them. It is the therapy relation itself—insofar as the intimacy generates a host of emotional responses—that provides the map, as it were, for these paths to emerge.

The therapy relationship is a unique one in that its purpose is not reproduced in other relationships (friendships, love affairs, or family). It gives the client a consistent and *current* experience of relating. We stress that this relationship is a real one and that the most meaningful moments in therapy take place when that realness is acknowledged and felt between client and therapist. By real relationship we mean that there are genuine feelings between the two people engaged in the process of the therapy. The therapist is there in a different capacity than her client, and it is the client's emotional life which receives the attention and analysis. There are feelings of concern, love, and empathy that build over the time together, and to call it merely a professional relationship gives it overtones of clinical sterility which misrepresents the human exchange of feelings and care in the room. Equally, it is not merely a transference relationship where the therapist represents others outside of the therapy room. Transference occurs within the relationship and transference interpretations can be useful at times. But most important is that there are two people in a special kind of relationship where the understanding is that one is there in an informed and caring capacity for the other.

In the therapy relationship communication takes place in both verbal and nonverbal ways. The therapist's dialogue with the client is an attempt to meet, in the sense of connect with, the client, to take in what the client is saying and to respond in such a way that she is letting the client know that she understands what it is the client is talking about. Questions are asked by the therapist with the aim first of seeking clearer understanding, thereby enabling a deeper connection, and second as a means for the therapist to touch on and open new psychological terrain with her client.

For the woman client, therapy may be an experience in which she feels both excitement and hope that here, at last, is someone who understands her. At the same time there is an underlying anxiety that accompanies her developing vulnerability in this relationship. The feminist therapist is aware of this vulnerability and attempts to make contact with the little-girl inside her client with a kind of consistent communication to that part of her psyche. Every communication and contact made with the little-girl inside is an essential step in the process of a feminist therapy.

Over the course of the therapy relationship, the therapist has in mind the deepening relationship she has with this once-hidden part of the psyche.

The client's feelings of self-hatred and self-deprecation ease as she experiences the acceptance and support of the therapist. Together they have tried to understand why the woman came to feel these things about herself in the first place and why she suffered such deep feelings of rejection and unworthiness. With each piece of understanding and acceptance comes an internal sense of confidence and substance. The woman may no longer fear being empty inside for she no longer is unable to contact that part of herself which was split off and repressed. In addition, as the therapy progresses the client takes in the care of the therapist. This internalization of the other (who is a separate woman with boundaries) and of the consistency in their relationship nourishes the little-girl inside just as consistent care and love is the food for the developing psyche of an infant. The client begins to embody the goodness and strength which she feels her therapist possesses. It becomes a part of her own sense of self and enhances her new feelings of substance. Over the course of the therapy the little-girl inside is less hidden and the woman begins to feel more accepting of herself as she feels accepted by her therapist. This is a fundamental challenge to the psychic construction of femininity. As such it is exciting and yet not unproblematic.

A phenomenon that we come across regularly in therapy is the difficulty that women have in taking in the care of the therapist. There is often anxiety that accompanies a sense of "getting better." Taking in the person of the therapist touches the deeply painful feelings of deprivation which the client feels, and so pain and associations of loss often follow those powerful moments of shared recognition of the therapist's care for the client. At a certain point in the therapy process the associations of loss that follow experiences of "getting" become defenses within themselves. In other words, the continual reminder of rejection and vulnerability become a block against taking in, consolidating change, trusting the substantive love that is now offered and internalized. The therapist must focus on the difficulties with "getting" in the therapy. The client inevitably feels frightened that if she really lets her therapist in, then she will lose the therapist or she will be abandoned. It is a struggle to trust that the care will remain with her always.

In addition, taking in the person of the therapist and feeling more whole within herself is problematic, for it may lead her to believe that she must give up her therapist. If she feels more substantive and less in need of the therapist to maintain a psychological wholeness for her, then she fears her connection to her therapist will be broken. Her history haunts her; separation is impossible. She cannot have herself and still have her caregiver. The idea of two separated, whole, and confident women who still have an attachment is so unknown. Her defenses come into the therapy this time to protect the relationship, to keep it going. She reassures her therapist that really it is not possible to manage on her own.

The client may fear that the therapist will not encourage or allow her feelings of autonomy and strength. The client unconsciously fears that this will be threatening to the therapist—just as it was to her mother. It is impossible to think that her therapist could take delight in her new feelings of self-confidence which enable her to venture farther and farther away, making new attachments in the world outside therapy. She may feel that she is abandoning her therapist and that, like her mother, the therapist will be left alone, bereft and needy. The separation and termination of the feminist therapy relationship is a delicate, complex, poignant, indeed profound experience between two women. The client has changed over the course of the relationship. She no longer feels a part of herself to be hidden from the world. She no longer feels that deep down she is still really a little girl with overwhelming and unending needs. She has felt supported, accepted, encouraged, and loved within the therapy relationship, and this has transformed the way she feels about herself. This, in turn, has dramatically changed the way she feels herself to be with other people—both women and men. She feels entitled to expect contact and nurturance on a regular basis and to not only provide to others. She is ready to leave therapy with a feeling of solidness within herself that she can rely on, and the security in feeling that another woman, her therapist, loves and respects her in her needs and in her autonomy.

REFERENCES

Baker, J. M. *Towards a new psychology of women*. Boston: Beacon Press, 1976.

Balint, M. *The basic fault: Therapeutic aspects of regression*. London: Tavistock, 1969.

Balikov, H. Fundamental impairment of the sensorium as a result of the normal adaptive process. *The Psychoanalytic Study of the Child*, 1960, *15*, 235.

Belotti, E. G. *Little girls*. London: Writers and Readers, 1975.

Chodorow, N. *The reproduction of mothering: Psychoanalysis and the sociology of gender*. Berkeley: University of California Press, 1978.

Eichenbaum, L., & Orbach, S. *Understanding women: A feminist psychoanalytic approach*. New York: Basic Books, 1983. (a)

Eichenbaum, L., & Orbach, S. *What do women want—exploding the myth of dependency*. New York: Putnam, 1983. (b)

Fairbairn, W. *Psychoanalytic studies of the personality*. London: Routledge & Kegan Paul, 1952.

Guntrip, H. *Schizoid phenomena and object relations theory*. London: Hogarth Press, 1968.

Guntrip, H. *Your mind and your health*. London: Unwin, 1970.

Klein, M. *Envy and gratitude*. London: Hogarth Press, 1975.

Mahler, M., Pine, F., & Bergman, A. *The psychological birth of the human infant: Symbiosis and individuation*. New York: Basic Books, 1975.

Mitchell, J. *Psychoanalysis and feminism*. New York: Pantheon Books, 1975.

Money, J., & Erhardt, A. *A man and woman, boy and girl: The differentiation and dimorphism of gender identity from conception to maturity*. Baltimore: Johns Hopkins University Press, 1972.

Spitz, R. *The first year of life: A psychoanalytic study of normal and deviant development of object relations*. New York: International Universities Press, 1965.

Stoller, R. *Sex and gender: On the development of masculinity and femininity*. New York: Jason Aronson, 1969.

Winnicott, D. W. *Collected papers through pediatrics to psychoanalysis*. London: Tavistock, 1958.

Winnicott, D. W. *The maturational processes and the facilitating environment*. New York: International Universities Press, Inc., 1965.

5

Female Role Socialization: The Analyst and the Analysis

BARBARA COHN SCHLACHET

There has been a good deal written on the impact of the differential socialization of women and men on the development of personality, character traits, styles of relating, and sense of self in relation to the world. There has also been much discussion of the impact of this for women who come for psychoanalytic and psychotherapeutic treatment, and what this means in working with women. What has been given little attention is the impact of gender socialization on the analyst, who comes to the analytic or therapeutic situation as a product of her or his own internalization of gender role socialization as a woman or as a man. This has implications not only for the experiences and values that the analyst brings to and communicates to her or his patients, and on the theoretical aspects of the analyst's work, but also, if we are to take account of feminist theory and research, on the interpersonal process of analysis and psychotherapy itself.

WOMEN'S SOCIALIZATION FOR
SEPARATING AND DIFFERENTIATING

A review of the feminist literature indicates that, because of the differential socialization of women and of men, their styles of relating to other people, to ideas, to the world at large are different. Chodorow (1978) states that "women, as mothers, produce daughters with mothering capacities and desire to mother. These capacities and needs grow out of the mother–daughter relationship itself. By contrast, women as mothers (and men as non-mothers) produce sons whose nurturant capacities and needs have been systematically curtailed and repressed" (p. 7). Because girls' identities are continuous with that of the person who is usually the primary parent and first love object, the mother, Chodorow claims that little girls tend to remain part of the mother–daughter dyad, while boys are more likely to curtail their love ties with their mothers. Because of this, girls do not have to repress or give up so thoroughly their pre-oedipal attachments to their mothers and do not have to deny pre-oedipal relational modes in the same way and to the same extent that boys do. Thus, girls do not have to feel as threatened as boys when regression to these modes occurs. Chodorow believes that girls emerge from this early mother–daughter relationship with the basis for empathy as part of their primary self-definition in a way that boys do not. She claims that, from very early on, because girls are parented by a person of the same gender, "girls come to experience themselves as less differentiated than boys, as more continuous with and related to the external object-world and as differently oriented to their inner objects as well" (Chodorow, 1978, p. 167). She sees women's object-worlds as becoming a more complex relational constellation than that of men, insofar as it does not entail the giving up of one parent (the mother) but, instead, the expansion of her world to include another parent and another mode of relating. Chodorow states that women's mothering

produces asymmetries in the relational experiences of girls and boys as they grow up, which account for crucial differences in the feminine and masculine personality, and the relational capacities and modes which they entail. Women and men grow up with personalities affected by different boundaries and experiences and differently constructed and experienced inner object-worlds, and are preoccupied with different relational issues. Feminine personality comes to be based less on repressions of inner objects, and fixed and firm splits in the ego, and more on retention and continuity of external relationships. From the retention of pre-oedipal attachments to their mother, growing girls come to define and experience themselves as continuous with others; their experience of self contains more flexible or permeable ego-boundaries. Boys come to define themselves as more separate and distinct, with a greater sense of rigid ego-boundaries and differentiation. *The basic feminine sense of self is connected to the world, the basic masculine sense of self is separate* (italics mine; 1978, p. 169).

She goes on to say that this often produces problems for women in separating and differentiating themselves, for men in intimacy.

Chodorow's view is supported by Gilligan's research. Gilligan (1982), in critiquing Kohlberg's work on morality, in which women attained no higher than stage three in Kohlberg's six-stage scale (six being the highest form of morality, abstract morality), notes that psychologists have been unable to understand female psychology because they have repeatedly tried to treat women as though they were men. Developmental theories have been built on studies and observations of men's lives and, when women fail to develop in the same way, have concluded that something must be wrong with women. Gilligan argues that something must, rather, be wrong with theory. Her point is that males and females develop differently, and that neither has failed if it has not become the other. For example, she speaks about the way that relationships, particularly around issues of dependency and individuation, are experienced differently by women and men. She states that,

> For boys and men separation and individuation are critically tied to gender identity since separation from the mother is essential for the development of masculinity. For girls and women, issues of femininity or feminine identity do not depend on the achievement of separation or on the process of individuation. Since masculinity is defined through separation while female identity is defined through attachment, male gender identity is threatened by intimacy while female gender identity is threatened by separation. Thus males tend to have difficulty with relationships, while females tend to have problems with individuation (p. 8).

She comments, however, that when the milestones of childhood and adolescent development in the psychological literature are markers of increasing separation, then women's failure to separate becomes, by definition, a failure to develop. According to Gilligan, "it appears that men and women may experience attachment and separation in different ways and that each sex perceives a danger which the other does not see . . . men in connection, women in separation" (p. 42).

DIFFERENCES IN PERSONALITY AND RELATIONAL STYLE

What happens, then, to these differences in personality and relational style when we become analysts and therapists? Do they go away as a function of our having been well analyzed? On the contrary, the hallmark of a "good" analysis has been, and continues in traditional circles to be, the establishment of a secure gender identity and gender role. Broverman's work (Broverman, Broverman, Clarkson, Rosenkrantz, & Vogel, 1970; Broverman, Vogel, Broverman, Clarkson, & Rosenkrantz, 1972) on sex-role stereotypes and clinical judgments of mental health illustrates the extent to which mental health practitioners differentiate between what is healthy for men and what is healthy for women, and the extent to which they see the former as congruent with what is deemed healthy in adults where sex is unspecified. According to Broverman's findings, then, analytic success would be demonstrated by women who exhibit feminine gender role characteristics and men who exhibit those deemed masculine. If we as analysts emerge from our own analyses as "well gendered" individuals, we need to explore the impact of this for our own analytic and therapeutic work with patients. We may see the patient differently, and have different goals and expectations because she or he is female or male, but we must also ask who it is that we bring into the consulting room with the patient, and whether the gender-related style of interacting of that person affects the treatment.

Several important issues arise here, some having to do with the analyst's relational style, and some having to do with her or his way of viewing the world, as psychoanalytic theory and training encourages a phallocentric perspective in which male development and behavior is the norm from which all else deviates.

In the first place, it becomes necessary to question whether psychoanalysis and psychoanalytically based psychotherapy emulate a male model of relating. Traditionally, male authorities have been mysterious, enigmatic others upon whose face one dares not look, and whose motives one would be presumptuous to question. In Western societies, as well as some Eastern societies, this characterizes the relationship between people and most of the deities that they worship, as well as with the representatives of those deities in most major institutions of worship. It is as if, if one did look upon the face of the powerful male authority, as Dorothy did in *The Wizard of Oz*, and see that he is mortal, he would lose all of his magical powers to protect and make better. To a certain extent, this model characterizes relationships between benevolent authorities and their charges, between gurus and their disciples, heads of state and their populace, physicians and their patients, parents and their small children, teachers and their students. Every analyst has some horror story about meeting up with a patient when the analyst's child is having a temper tantrum at the zoo, or of being seen somewhat inebriated at a party. What makes these horror stories? Is it that the analyst has been seen as a mortal, and, if so, why is this such a horror? Perhaps it has to do with our dread of our mortality, and our need to see our authorities as immortal, not of the earthly and fleshly world, as Rank (1958), Becker (1973), and Dinnerstein (1976) suggest. Women, as representatives of the flesh—it is from the mortal flesh of a woman that each of us is born, and her body is a constant reminder of that fact—cannot fulfill this need for the denial of mortality, except where her fleshly qualities are renounced, as they are by women in religious life in some denominations. This historical relation to woman's body as both worshiped and despised for its fecund and earthly qualities is beyond the scope of this paper, but it has been the subject of much interdisciplinary speculation and study. If our strong wish is for an authority to be able to allay our fears of mortality by his separateness from the flesh, what impact does this have for women as experts? Our being women means that we can only make the overt claim to be able to help with the problem for which our expertise is being sought; we cannot in any way meet the covert need of being able to save in a larger sense—to keep safe, to save from mortality.

The analytic relationship is certainly a hierarchical one, based on a relationship between a benevolent authority, an expert, and a person in need of help, who purchases the authority's expertise. The authority establishes the rules of the relationship, both practical and relational: who tells what, whose life becomes known. The expectation is that the patient will become more involved with the analyst than vice versa. The analyst is not required to make self-disclosures (in fact, this is discouraged, sometimes to the point of analyzing, rather than answering requests for information about the facts of the analyst's professional qualifications). This is certainly not the way that women have related to other women, not even in expert–novice or expert–client relationships. Women have most often related to one another out of a sense of continuity and shared experience, where learning has been more of an apprenticeship kind of learning than a learning of roles. It is interesting to note in this context that the literature shows repeatedly that modeling, including some self-disclosure on the part of women therapists, has had a positive effect on client self-disclosure (Krumholtz, Becker-Haven, & Burnett, 1979; Lerman, 1976). The importance of identification and the communality of experience that women share with other women for therapeutic outcome has also been demonstrated (Jeske, 1973; Krause, 1971; Kravetz, 1978; Mander & Rush, 1974).

As women analysts we learn the same theory in the same training institutes as our male colleagues do, yet our relational styles and experiences are very different from theirs. It would seem that this would have to impact on our clinical work, on the degree to which we adhere to prescribed analytic roles, and on our feelings about accepting or not accepting these roles. Perhaps one of the reasons that we so often feel like imposters as analysts and therapists is precisely because we relate in similar manner to our patients as we do to other people in our lives; that is, we are women first and professionals second. We are women who, in the context of a professional relationship, bring our professional expertise into a situation. We are not being "like analysts"; we are being women who are analysts. This works out more easily if we are dentists, or gynecologists, that is, if the helping service that we provide is concretely different from, while being embedded in, a relational context. As analysts and therapists, however, the relational context *is*, in many ways, the helping situation. Thus, if we don't make that context different from the context of other relationships in our lives, are we, in fact, doing anything *real?* This is even more complicated by the fact that as women we tend to devalue our empathic, understanding, "emotional" qualities under any circumstances, as does the larger culture, so that, if we're relating as women it is, by definition, deficient. (See Margaret Gibbs' chapter in this book for a parallel discussion of why women therapists feel like imposters in their professional role.)

This was brought home to me at a meeting that I attended in which a panel of three male analysts discussed the tribulations of psychoanalytic work and its hazardous effects on their home lives. I found myself feeling unduly irritated at their descriptions of the analyst's hard life, which I attributed to my own working-class background ("Coal miners work hard," I found myself muttering to my neighbor). It wasn't until later that day, in thinking about it, that I realized that they *were* working hard, at a task for which they hadn't been socialized; they were working all day (and perhaps evening) at listening to other people and trying to make sense of and empathize with those people's experiences, often different from their own. This was so clearly *work* to them, as opposed to what one might do on the telephone in the evening with a friend, or with a next-door neighbor who is in trouble, that there seemed to be no crisis of faith in charging a high fee for the activity, or in feeling extraordinarily useful. One could wonder whether women analysts and therapists adhere to the male relational model in analysis in order to give ourselves a similar kind of support—that this is work, it is different from what we usually do in relationships. Perhaps our analytic and therapeutic skills and training, no matter how extensive, are not sufficient to do this for us.

The issue of modeling enters into our work as women analysts in yet another sense, having to do with the messages that we intentionally and unintentionally transmit about women to our patients by our own behavior in and around the analytic work. Discussion with my own female and male colleagues indicates that the women analysts that I know have more difficulty in refusing to schedule an extra hour in an already overscheduled day when somebody is in distress than do male therapists of my acquaintance. Without making a judgment about whether either of these modes is the "better" one, it should be noted that the women analysts behave more in keeping with the assumption about women in the larger culture—that we are always available to be nurturing. Perhaps our patients' response to our refusal would also be different than if it were given by a male analyst. It may also be that our unwillingness to be seen as "not giving" and "not nice" enters into our work in, for example, influencing the degree to which we are willing to confront and arouse anger, or in issues of fee setting and payment of fees. It is important to consider the implications of these gender-role messages for our patients who are trying to grapple with the same issues: women with how they see themselves, and men with how they see themselves in relation to women.

GENDER DIFFERENCES IN TRANSFERENCE ISSUES

The differential socialization of women and men unquestionably plays a role in transference and countertransference issues in the analytic situation. We must wonder, for example, whether the analytic situation cultivates a highly charged erotic transference between male analysts and female patients because it closely approximates what is idealized for male–female relationships in the culture, an ideal based on a father–daughter relationship, i.e., a more powerful man helping a more dependent woman. This is a more erotically charged cultural ideal than the converse, a more powerful woman with a more dependent man, although the latter can certainly give rise to other kinds of feelings. To what degree does the fantasy of male power and omnipotence enter into the transference, and what is the impact of this, or its absence, in transference relationships with female analysts? We also have to ask what the differential impact of an eroticized transference is on male and female analysts, given their different backgrounds and experiences. Is an eroticized transference more threatening to a woman analyst when coming from a male patient, when her experience with unsolicited male sexuality has trained her to react defensively, be wary of physical danger that can be all too real, and be sure that in some way she's not "asking for it"? Since the analyst is always "asking for it"—i.e., not discouraging sexual feelings as women are supposed to do—this becomes quite dissonant with the woman analyst's gender-role training.

We would none of us agree that an analyst or therapist need have the same experiences as her or his patient in order to understand the latter. Sometimes this helps, sometimes it actually gets in the way, as when we assume that, for example, because we and the patient experienced the same event we, therefore, have had the same experience. Having had what we presume to be the same experience can keep us from asking the questions that really define and delineate our patients' experience. What makes us effective with any patient, whether from the same or another culture, is the degree to which we can recognize that that person's experience is unique and try to understand it as such. In addition to its being personally unique, however, we have to make an effort to understand the cultural framework in which the experience took place in order to understand its meaning for our patients. This, I believe, is where psychoanalysis runs into trouble in theorizing about and working with women patients, as well as with other groups who are not part of the dominant culture. It is also where we run into difficulty in training, and in being analysts, as we do not articulate the developmental and characterological differences between ourselves and our male colleagues. We behave, in fact, as though the only differences between patients are those involving diagnostic and prognostic categories, and the only differences between analysts are schools of psychoanalytic thought and expertise.

Our assumption that women are part of the dominant culture leads us to misinterpret the nature of women's experience. Without the understanding that from the moment of birth boys and girls (including those who grow up to be analysts and therapists) are wrapped in different colors, handled in different ways, responded to differentially by parents of both sexes, as well as by neighbors, teachers, playmates, bought different toys and read different books, permitted and forbidden to do different things, faced with different expectations about how they grow up and what they will grow up to be, occupationally and characterologically—without the understanding that boys and girls, men and women are, in fact, *other* to one another in more than biological terms, there can be no way of understanding the impact of this differential socialization on ourselves, our patients, and our work. A feminist psychoanalysis must make this assumption of otherness, whether we be women working with women or with men, or whether we be men working with patients of either sex. The interaction between ourselves and our patients cannot be understood without an understanding of what our own gender socialization brings to the interaction. In this way it will be possible for us, as women analysts, to reinvent our role in the analysis, to explore how we can work most productively as analysts who are women, and to contribute to the critique and reformulation of psychoanalytic theory and practice.

REFERENCES

Becker, E. *The denial of death*. New York: The Free Press, 1973.

Broverman, I. K., Broverman, D. M., Clarkson, F. L., Rosenkrantz, P., & Vogel, S. R. Sex role stereotypes and clinical judgments of mental health. *Journal of Consulting and Clinical Psychology*, 1970, *34*, 1–7.

Broverman, I., Vogel, D., Broverman, D., Clarkson, F., and Rosenkrantz, P. Sex-role stereotypes: a current appraisal. *Journal of Social Issues*, 1972, *28*, 59–78.

Chodorow, N. *The reproduction of mothering*. Berkeley: University of California Press, 1978.

Dinnerstein, D. *The mermaid and the minotaur: Sexual arrangements and human malaise*. New York: Harper & Row, 1976.

Gilligan, C. *In a different voice*. Cambridge: Harvard University Press, 1982.

Jeske, J. O. Identification and therapeutic effects in group therapy. *Journal of Counseling Psychology*, 1973, *20*, 528–530.

Krause, C. The femininity complex and women therapists. *Journal of Marriage and the Family*, 1971, *33*, 476–482.

Kravetz, D. Consciousness-raising groups in the 1970's. *Psychology of Women Quarterly,* 1978, *3,* 168–186.

Krumholtz, J. D., Becker-Haven, J. F., & Burnett, K. F. Counseling psychology. *Annual Review of Psychology,* 1979, *30,* 555–602.

Lerman, H. What happens in feminist therapy. In S. Cox (Ed.), *Female psychology: The emerging self.* Chicago: Scientific Research Associates, 1976.

Mander, A. V., & Rush, A. K. *Feminism as therapy.* New York: Random House, 1974.

Rank, O. *Beyond psychology.* New York: Dover Books, 1958.

■ three
FEMINIST THERAPY: TREATMENT STRATEGIES

■ 6

Treatment of the Impostor Phenomenon in High-Achieving Women

SUZANNE IMES AND PAULINE ROSE CLANCE

We have coined the term *impostor phenomenon* to describe an internal experience of phoniness common among high-achieving women who persist in believing they are not bright, capable, or creative, despite ample evidence to the contrary. While others are praising their accomplishments, they are secretly convinced that they have fooled all those who commend them. Living with a fear that they will eventually be "found out," they suffer high degrees of anxiety in their strivings to achieve standards of excellence sufficient to hide their assumed inadequacies from others. Self-declared impostors are highly motivated to achieve and can often push through their fears and self-doubts to produce superior work, get promotions, attain advanced degrees, and so on. When they do succeed, however, they fail to feel a sustained sense of personal pride in their accomplishments, for they negate their abilities by attributing their successes to factors beyond their control, such as overevaluation of their work by others, or the results of hard work which they are not convinced they can repeat in the future. They also discount their abilities by believing that people who praise them are actually responding positively only to their charm, sensitivity, or other interpersonal skills. With each new assignment, task, or challenge, the fear emerges anew, "This time I can't do it. This time I will be found out."

If women with impostor feelings more often than not appear to be succeeding, then why are we concerned with "treatment"? What might a therapist have to offer someone who might be every bit as accomplished as herself, or at least clearly proceeding along a course of achievement? If one goal of feminist therapy is empowerment, then we definitely have something valuable to offer. The self-appointed impostor suffers from lack of a solid, realistic sense of her own capabilities. She is *not* fully empowered to own her strengths, to accept her deficits, or to function self-assuredly. Anxiety, self-doubts, fear of failure, fear of success, and worry about not living up to others' expectations all operate insidiously to undermine her ability to function out of a space of centeredness and free flowing energy and toward pleasure rather than pain. She looks to mentors to validate the strengths she hopes must be there and is repeatedly disappointed because she is not able to internalize the validation she receives. She demands perfection of herself and is then necessarily doomed to feel dissatisfaction. This self-dissatisfaction affects her internal state as well as her personal and professional relationships and her productivity. Thus, the impostor phenomenon cannot be viewed narrowly by the therapist as a single "symptom" to be "fixed" or gotten rid of. The therapist must view it from a broader, multilevel perspective, taking into consideration original family dynamics and influences and how they are currently interfacing with the client's personal and professional relationships and societal expectations.

In this chapter, we will be discussing some specific strategies of working with clients who display one or more of the impostor characteristics or behaviors. Yet these specific methods are utilized within the context of good psychotherapy, involving an empathic, supportive, and nonauthoritarian relationship with the client. Our therapeutic goals are to enable the client to move toward her own self-actualization and to assist her to attain her own achievement aspirations. We see the therapy process as an empowerment process wherein the client is able to expand the number of options that are open to her for effective living. Essentially, we work within an organismic model which emphasizes the development of the self-regulation of the organism. More specifically, from a gestalt therapy point of view, we believe that quality of life is impeded when parts of the self are disowned. Unfinished experiences in the past and fears about the future interfere with lively, energetic, joyful experiencing of the now (see Polster & Polster, 1973). In the case of the impostor phenomenon, the person has disowned her capability, intelligence, and creativity and is unable to participate fully in and make contact with the experience of accomplishing something important to her.

In the context of this basic model, we employ approaches from other therapies to help the client bring into awareness what modes of feeling, thinking, and experiencing are getting in the way of being empowered.

THE EMERGENCE OF THE IMPOSTOR PHENOMENON: RECOGNITION OF THE IMPOSTOR PHENOMENON BY THE THERAPIST

Our clients do not often come into therapy with impostor feelings as a presenting problem. They are much more likely to come in feeling overwhelmed, tense, depressed, or dissatisfied with themselves. Then, as they deal with these symptoms or issues, impostor feelings emerge. The impostor phenomenon is rarely in the conscious awareness or control of the individual. The client does not come into therapy saying, "I feel like an impostor and want help with it." Rather, she experiences the effects of the impostor phenomenon, such as feeling anxious about completing a task, being immobilized in the midst of trying to accomplish the task, being down on herself for not being able to do it in the manner she thinks she ought to, or even feeling sheer terror that she simply cannot do it. With each new challenge, the client is convinced that she will finally be exposed as a fraud. At the same time she feels driven to do well, to succeed, to prove to herself and others that she really is capable.

A case example is as follows: A client whom we shall call Patricia has a B.S. in nursing and has been working in a state agency. She is dissatisfied with her present job and is discussing her options with her therapist. Her dissatisfaction is mainly arising because she is very bright and wants to try out new ideas and projects, but she does not have a high enough position in the hierarchy to do so. She knows she needs more education to get the position she wants and is considering the possibility of getting an M.A. in nursing. Yet, it is clear to the therapist that she probably needs an M.D. to pursue her interests. Gradually, it emerged in the therapy that she was so underestimating her own abilities that she was not even considering the option of obtaining an M.D. She was experiencing the impostor phenomenon without realizing it. When the therapist raised the possibility of her obtaining an M.D., impostor feelings emerged and needed to be dealt with.

Another example is that of Grace, a chemistry major in a prestigious liberal arts college. Grace was asked to do honors work by her department chair. She refused because she honestly believed she lacked the ability. Yet all objective evidence indicated that she would do excellent work. As she discussed her decision, many impostor feelings emerged. The faculty of her department select students who have done excellent work and whom they believe to have outstanding abilities. Yet Grace honestly thought that if she did honors, she would not succeed this time. She expected that under close supervision her inadequacies would emerge.

One task for the therapist at such junctures in therapy is to recognize when dilemmas and behaviors typical of the impostor phenomenon are occurring. Impostor feelings frequently underlie what at first sounds like a situation that requires mere problem solving. The client may be setting goals that reflect an underestimation of her abilities, such as Patricia was doing. If the therapist had not recognized the potential impostor feelings, she might have tried to help solve Patricia's problem by encouraging her to try for her M.A. in nursing or assisting her in deciding when and how to apply to which schools.

The therapist is wise to suspect underlying impostor feelings when a bright, heretofore high-achieving client, such as Grace, chooses to avoid an achievement challenge altogether. In Grace's case, the therapist might have been tempted to respect her decision not to pursue honors work before fully exploring the basis of it. Or she might have wanted to convince Grace that she could do honors by pointing out her past successes and giving encouragement. This latter approach is often useful to clients, but not until they have explored their impostor feelings and at least have reached a cognitive understanding that their doubts about their abilities are not based in reality.

Other clues that the impostor phenomenon is operating in a client include vague fears about not being able to accomplish a given assignment or project, procrastinating or not seeming to have enough energy to complete an important task, or experiencing anxiety in the process of achieving a goal. The impostor phenomenon may be a factor even farther

from conscious awareness in some very capable clients who avoid bringing up achievement-related issues in therapy altogether and use all of
their energy in and out of therapy focusing on family or relationship
issues.

TAKING THE CLIENT'S DOUBTS
AND FEARS SERIOUSLY

The most critical task for the therapist when impostor feelings emerge is to
take the client's doubts seriously and to hear carefully what she has to say
about them. Too often in the past, if the client has dared to share her
doubts, friends, teachers, family members, or employers have hastened to
reassure her, "Don't worry. You'll do fine. There's no problem because you
always do well." In these reassurances, people have discounted her feelings and have not heard the nature of her fears. As a result of these
discounts, individuals often cease to express their doubts openly. Thus,
they go "undercover" with their fears and cut off the possibility of being
understood. For example, one client remembered her despair when, at
the age of 15, she failed her driver's license test and was scared she would
fail again the next time she took it. Her mother responded by saying,
"Don't be upset; it's not the end of the world. You'll do fine the next time."
The client kept subsequent fears about failing to herself until she got
into therapy and had experienced acceptance from a nonjudgmental
therapist.

The therapist can show that she is taking the client's doubts and fears
seriously by thoroughly exploring the nature of these doubts and fears and
by obtaining specific information about them. She needs to ask such
questions as, "What are your doubts in this situation?" "What may happen
if you fail to do this the way you want to do it?" "How may it happen?"
"What are you saying to yourself about this exam, paper, or other project?"
A case illustration follows:

Jane recently returned to the university to obtain a B.A., after having
worked for several years. Her grades during her first two years of college
were excellent. She is now in an individualized independent study program in which she can receive university credits for her life experience if
she can write a paper demonstrating the knowledge she gained in her
work. A faculty committee will evaluate her paper and assign her from one
to four quarters of credit, based on the paper's merit. Jane feels stuck and
unable to write the paper. It was due a quarter ago, and she has been

putting it off. Whenever she tries to start writing, she finds herself saying that it won't be good enough and that she doesn't know enough.

When Jane's therapist asks her about her experience with writing papers in the past, Jane acknowledges that she has always done well and received good grades and good evaluations from her professors. But Jane attributes this success to her ability to "appear to know more than I do" and to "make it look good on the surface." Without denying this self-description, the therapist inquires what keeps Jane from repeating the performance. Jane replies that this time, the project is so important that she won't be able to "get away with a surface impression."

The therapist reminds Jane that, in their conversations, Jane has talked about her work experience, and that the therapist has learned a lot from Jane. "Of course," adds the therapist, "You could be fooling me, too." Jane acknowledges that she does know a little; but "there's a lot I don't know." The therapist then asks whether Jane's professors expect her to know everything about her subject. Jane admits that they do not. "But," she adds, "*I* expect me to know it all."

Jane, however, has begun to realize that she does not have to know everything, or to put everything into her paper. The therapist assures her that her faculty members do not expect her to write a book, but rather to demonstrate that she has the information critical to an understanding of her subject, and that she can analyze and evaluate it and show how it relates to her experience. Jane begins to feel that she can start to work.

The therapist underscores her confidence in Jane's ability by saying, "Jane, I know you've been feeling that you just can't do it this time. . . . I also heard you say that you have . . . always done well. So I believe you can repeat what you've always done in the past this time, but I want us to explore how these feelings emerge in you and where they originated." Jane assents.

In this case illustration, the therapist checks out the objective data about Jane's past experience with writing papers; yet she also takes Jane's doubts seriously and thus enables her to express her feelings, to see the underlying beliefs that lead to her anxiety and immobilization, and to begin to question the reality of her doubts. After this session, Jane was able to begin working on her paper. We have often noticed that just being able to talk about such fears enables clients to feel relieved. Yet the therapist must *hear* empathically the client's subjective belief that she *will* not do well this time if she is to get beyond this belief.

EXAMINING FAMILY DYNAMICS
AND SCRIPT MESSAGES

We have discussed in an earlier article (Clance & Imes, 1978) typical family dynamics of self-defined impostors. Clients in the early phases of therapy often are not conscious of the degree to which they are basing their perceptions of themselves on early family messages, script decisions, and designated role in the family. Early script messages about their intellect are accepted as the truth. Therefore it is crucial for the therapist to help the client discover, become aware of, and undo the family myth. It is important to obtain a detailed, thorough family history. Adlerian life-style questionnaires (Ansbacher & Ansbacher, 1956) or Transactional Analysis script analysis procedures (Steiner, 1974) can be useful in this phase of therapy.

From the Adlerian model we have adapted and found the following questions particularly useful: When you were in grade school, which of the members of your family was considered most intelligent? Who was most creative? Who was most sensitive? Who was most charming? Who made the best grades? For later years we ask: Who is considered most successful as an adult? Who's considered most intelligent as an adult? Who has obtained the highest level of education? Who has been most successful in his or her chosen field?

From answers to these questions the client can begin to recognize early script messages and decisions. After much therapeutic work she can begin to see that the family members, including herself, have agreed on the client's role in the family, and she can begin to release herself from this role.

Women with impostor feelings often have a family member (most frequently a sibling) who is considered the "bright one" in the family. In such a family the client is often the "charming" or "sensitive one."

In Donna's family, her mother was seen to have taken *all* the honors—brains, charm, perceptiveness. Donna has a Master's degree in counseling and has always done well in school and in various jobs she has held. She has never experienced a significant failure in school or on the job. She is currently considering changing careers entirely and starting her own catering business. Although she is excited about the new venture, she is terrified to carry through with it for fear she will fail.

Her therapist could certainly empathize with Donna's fears about starting something entirely new and first assisted her in considering whether she actually had the capability and resources necessary to succeed in the new business she was planning. After ascertaining that with some time and effort it was realistic for Donna to proceed, she had one last fear:

> **Donna:** You know, I hate to admit this, but I'm even worried I can't do the part of this business I know I would be best at, and that's actually preparing the food.
>
> **Therapist:** Are you a good cook?
>
> **Donna:** (Sheepishly) Well—yes—I guess—I *think* I am.
>
> **Therapist:** What is your hesitation?
>
> **Donna:** Well, I know I can cook okay, but I don't think I can put it all together and then make it look all good together.
>
> **Therapist:** By whose standards?
>
> **Donna:** Ah ha! It's my mother again. If I can't even do that as well as she can, then there's *nothing* I can compare with her on. She's better at everything.
>
> **Therapist:** Is that really true?
>
> **Donna:** She's definitely more charming and can mix with people more easily than I can.
>
> **Therapist:** Has she ever started a catering business and had to put food together tastefully and decoratively?
>
> **Donna:** Well, no, but when she serves a meal, it's always beautifully done. But come to think of it, I always get a lot of compliments when I give a dinner party too.
>
> **Therapist:** So maybe you have a style of entertaining that may be *different* from your mother's but not necessarily less effective?
>
> **Donna:** That could be. I've always considered her way better and put myself down.

Once Donna realized that mother's superiority was a family myth rather than a reality written in stone, she could look at her *own* skills realistically and value them as being different from instead of inferior to her mother's. After this session, Donna's anxiety subsided, and she made a plan for learning the components of the business one at a time.

Examining family origins is also vitally important for those clients who were told in the beginning of their young lives that they were supremely intelligent and could accomplish any intellectual or creative task with ease. These clients were scripted as the "bright one" in the family and have always felt that they must live up to expectations of perfection in order to continue to win familial approval and acceptance. Having internalized their parents' unreachable standards of excellence, they begin to doubt their inherent intellectual ability whenever they encounter difficulty in initiating or accomplishing a challenging goal. They are confused about the image of "perfection with ease" that has been perpetrated on them in contrast to their experience of having to work hard to accomplish some tasks and making some mistakes in the process. They conclude that their parents must be wrong and illogically jump to the conclusion that they must be fooling their parents.

A client who has been designated the "bright one" in the family may be aware of her current fears and self-doubts, but she is often not consciously aware of the early roots of the conclusions she drew about her abilities. The therapist can help her face the process of this early decision and to demythologize the idea that intelligence means "accomplishment with ease." The therapist can also help her see the illogic in her decision that she is an intellectual fraud, develop a realistic view of her intellectual strengths, and accept her weaknesses without discounting her overall superior intellectual functioning.

We begin to get clues that the child was operating within this particular family system when we ask, for example, "How did your family respond when you brought your school projects and papers home?" The parents reply, "This is wonderful work. You always do well. Of course we knew you would." Or less verbal parents might simply nod, as if to say, "Good. Of course we expected this from you."

Early childhood stories often confirm that the precocious child script had even earlier foundations. When we ask, "What stories did your parents tell you about what you were like as a very young child?", these stories abound with high praises of their early accomplishments, such as saying intelligible words at six months of age and saying complete sentences by their first birthday, or reciting nursery rhymes before most children can talk.

The client interprets such stories to mean that she must forever live up to this "genius" script, at first in order to continue to gain parental approval, and in later years to obtain self-approval and to avoid criticism. The therapist works with the client to remember these early childhood script messages, to identify the injunctions the messages contain, and to see how the injunctions have affected her in the past and continue to interfere with her current functioning.

Cynthia's parents were of the head-nodding type. The injunction was, "Being bright is a condition of being a member of this family. No failures will be allowed or acknowledged. In addition, you must be successful in all areas of endeavor." The pervasiveness of this family message is starkly illustrated by Cynthia's memory of an interaction with her sister when Cynthia was six years old. The two were watching TV together, and when Cynthia admitted that she did not know who President Eisenhower was, her sister told her that the police would put Cynthia in jail for not knowing such a thing.

Feeling great pressure to succeed academically, Cynthia put all of her effort into her studies and avoided competitions such as debates, writing competitions, talent shows, and even class discussions which might reveal lack of perfect knowledge. In graduate school she refused to ask questions about topics she did not understand for fear of exposing what she considered her ignorance. She had a tendency to avoid competition with her colleagues and to avoid taking on challenges when she was not absolutely certain she had enough prior knowledge to succeed.

During the process of therapy, Cynthia has been able to reassess her family's values and beliefs about the nature of intelligence. She is learning that she can be very bright *and* still have unanswered questions *and* have difficulty completing some types of tasks. She is also learning that she does not have to be good at everything in order to acknowledge that she is indeed a very bright and talented person.

OTHER THERAPEUTIC INTERVENTIONS

We have used several therapeutic approaches concurrently in dealing with the impostor phenomenon and find that a combination of approaches works well. One gestalt approach we have used is to have the client imagine that all the people she thinks she has deceived are before her, and to tell them how she has conned or tricked them. Then she is to imagine out loud how each person would respond.

Another way to enable the client to touch base with reality, and one that we highly recommend, is to have her share her impostor feelings in a group therapy setting, especially one in which there are other high-achieving persons with similar feelings. Often realizing that one is not alone in having such impostor feelings brings great relief as well as the ability to begin to see oneself more realistically.

Another gestalt approach is to get the client to act out being bright in the presence of the group or the therapist. Responses to this exercise are varied. Some clients then become aware of another buried fantasy—one of being exceedingly special. This fantasy is often accompanied by its own fears and feelings of guilt. This exercise may also call up a client's hidden fears of success.

Another approach may be to have the client keep a feedback journal and record in it both the positive feedback she receives on her achievements and how she keeps herself from accepting it. For a woman who has used charm or intellectual flattery to gain approval, a strategy may be to become aware when she is being phony and become conscious of those times when she does say or do something she does not want to in order to get approval. Then she is encouraged to risk "being herself" and to see what happens.

One exercise that we have designed is a guided fantasy in which we ask the client to imagine that she is very successful, receiving public recognition for her accomplishments in her chosen field. Then she is asked to invite her parents and other significant people to be present, and to imagine their reactions. The reported reactions may be how the significant other might actually respond, or they may be the client's projections. What is critical is that the real or imagined responses be brought into conscious awareness. Then the therapist can work with the reactions in a variety of ways. The therapist may challenge the power that the client has given to these significant others. The client's ultimate catastrophic fear is often of the husband (parent, etc.) leaving or abandoning her. And in some cases where abandonment is a real possibility, women have to choose whether they want to continue on the road to success and face the consequences of losing someone very important.

Another response to the exercise might be an inability to imagine being successful at all. One client said that imagining herself as successful would mean to her that she was arrogant. As a paradoxical intervention, we might then ask her to take on an "arrogant" posture and brag about herself to us. She then gets in touch with the positive feelings of claiming her abilities and accomplishments. Reframing "arrogance" as "self-confidence" can make the owning of this part of the personality more palatable to some clients.

Guilt often emerges when clients fantasize themselves being successful. In her doctoral dissertation on the impostor phenomenon, Joan Harvey (1981) found that those subjects who reported that they had attained an educational level atypical of their families scored higher on an Impostor Phenomenon Scale. Lydia is a case in point. No one in her family had gone to college; moreover, she grew up in a mining community where doing well in school, pursuing creative or cultural interests, or even appearing bright were not valued. Although Lydia did manage to be graduated with honors from a prestigious northeastern university, she has since then been employed in jobs which have underutilized her abilities and has avoided applying to graduate school even though she says she would like to go on for a Ph.D. She fears thinking of herself as different from her family and community members, so she convinces herself that she is not different by thinking of herself as an impostor. She feels guilty whenever she even entertains fleeting thoughts that her success in college might have been attributable to anything other than luck and her ability to con professors.

In working with such a client, the therapist attempts to uncover what is involved in her guilt, whether it be a cover for resentment toward family and community members for not affirming her intelligence or a way to make up or "atone" for her greater achievements. Then the therapist helps the client examine how she is similar to as well as different from her family. The client does not want to be alienated from her original culture; therefore, by identifying with certain aspects of that environment, she can gradually feel better about accepting ways in which she is different.

DEALING WITH PERFECTIONISM

Perfectionism is a predominant theme for all the women with whom we have worked on impostor feelings. They set extremely high standards of performance for themselves, expecting to be productive, insightful and creative *all of the time*. Moreover, they tend to believe it could and should be possible to operate at such maximum capacity consistently. Anything less than complete knowledge of a subject, or doing any project less than exactly "right" is unacceptable and proof of their lack of worth. This attempt to be perfect gets in people's way and takes its toll in a number of ways. First, the agony of the process itself, the constant anxiety to which the woman subjects herself in her attempt to live up to her goal, is with her always. And, second, her attempt to be perfect keeps her from doing as much as she actually could. Thus, a double drain on her energy exists.

Each person has her own set of ideas about the "right way" to perform, and when she achieves anything less than this, she considers the enterprise to be a failure, which only provides further evidence of the client's presumed stupidity.

A client's perfectionism frequently involves the notion that whatever the client is weak in is what constitutes "real" intelligence. For example, a client who is good at remembering facts, and invariably does well on tests, may say that that ability is not "real" intelligence; "real" intelligence means being able to analyze, synthesize, and problem solve. The good problem solver, on the other hand, will believe the ability to amass huge quantities of facts is what constitutes real intelligence.

Related to this notion is the one that says that doing what one is good at does not count; what "counts" is doing what one finds hard. This message creates a double bind: What the client is good at and finds easy to do becomes discounted while what she finds more difficult becomes the test of her ability. She puts aside an interest or capability that she finds herself working at easily and well, and she goes after a task that she finds hard. Then when she finds it hard, she has renewed proof of her own lack of intelligence.

Clients go to great lengths to produce work of such excellence that no one in a position to judge the quality of the work could possibly consider them a failure. And in their frame of thinking anything less than perfection means failure. Thus, they push through periods of great anxiety and agonizing impasses to produce very high-quality work. Therapeutic intervention allows them to become aware of the power of the sheer terror involved in the possibility of failing. Moreover, such clients frequently are unable to discriminate between those tasks needing to be done with great perfection and those tasks which do not need perfection but only need to be done moderately well. They may put in as much work on a minor project as a major one. For example, they agonize over writing a memorandum as much as over writing a grant proposal.

The therapist needs to help such a client realize that her world will not fall apart even if she does work that is somewhat sloppy or less than her best. The therapist can work to have the client actively decide which projects require her best work versus those that do not.

A graduate student who was feeling overwhelmed in the process of writing her dissertation proposal typifies these aspects of the impostor phenomenon. She was stuck because she believed that every concept had to be perfectly thought out, every sentence had to be perfectly constructed, and all angles had to be covered. She failed to realize that the committee did not expect perfection at this point in the process.

In working with her we used humor, saying, "Why not let your committee work a little? They'll feel left out if they don't get to do something." She was surprised by the idea that they would want to help her. We also addressed her need to struggle for hours to create perfect sentences. We worked with her so she could write down anything that came to her mind when she was stuck and then proceed to the next sentence or idea. With these interventions, she was able to complete her proposal in less time and with less struggle and pain than was usual for her. This mode was reinforced for her when her committee responded positively to her proposal and provided productive ideas. Since she had accepted the idea that their role was to provide input rather than to expose her as a fraud, she did not feel inadequate for not producing a perfect document on the first try.

Our clients often think they should be experts in whatever they attempt *before* they even get started. Donna, the client who was considering starting a catering business, provides an example. Although Donna had extensively investigated the things she would have to know in the catering business, she continued to feel "overwhelmed" by all the things she did not yet know. Careful questioning by her therapist revealed that Donna had already lined up someone to help her in marketing and someone to do her accounting, and that she also had the names of two caterers she could call. Yet she had not called the caterers because, as she said, "I'm afraid they'll think I'm dumb." Her thorough preparations gave her no feelings of security at all.

We talked about how Donna was scaring and overwhelming herself by thinking she had to "know it all." By assuring her that it made no sense that she should know so much at this point and that she both had the time and could take the time to find out, she felt much relieved. Her anxiety subsided, and she could then get back in touch with her excitement and make a plan for learning the components of the business one at a time without being overwhelmed.

Another type of intervention may be to get a client to set limits on the amount of time she spends on a project or to risk handing in a project even though it seems imperfect to her so she can get realistic feedback. As a result, she can realize that other people's expectations are not nearly as high as her own. The graduate student did risk writing what she considered a "merely adequate" dissertation; her committee, however, praised her for outstanding work. This experience has led her to be less compulsive and perfectionistic on subsequent projects.

Another therapeutic issue underlying the perfectionism is the terror of failure. Often the client thinks she cannot tolerate failure—that she cannot live through a failure experience. She cannot imagine surviving serious criticism, much less really failing. Most clients initially cannot even verbalize the nature of this terror; therefore it is important for the therapist to assist the client in bringing the specific fears into conscious awareness. When the fears become conscious, the client can then realize the irrational nature of these fears. She comes to realize that one failure would not be catastrophic and that she could live through a failure.

DEALING WITH RESISTANCES

Although the specific strategies that we have outlined are effective in assisting clients in dealing with acute episodes of impostor feelings, the feelings usually reemerge in any new situation or setting that challenges intellect or creativity. To achieve any long-lasting effects of treatment, the therapy must address the client's resistances to internalizing success. Like any enduring behavior, impostor behaviors tend to last over time because they have apparent benefits for the clients. As we have pointed out previously (Clance & Imes, 1978), maintaining the impostor stance has resulted in a fair degree of success for clients and has prevented them from facing real or imagined negative consequences of owning their abilities.

Several themes emerge in our clients as they struggle with how very difficult it is to give up impostor attitudes and to replace them with a solid, realistic, and rewarding sense of their own abilities. Some women have the superstitious conviction that the cycle of anxiety, self-doubt, and compulsive hard work are actually necessary in order to succeed. They believe that

taking a more relaxed approach to work would result in failure and exposure of their inadequacies. Other women are afraid that if they were really
to believe they are intelligent, they and other people would expect more
from them than they are now producing. Since they are already working
very hard, they have the additional fear that they could not work even
harder or produce even more.

Inherent in maintaining impostor feelings is often fear of power.
Women have often not had opportunities to experience the benefits of
having a significant amount of power, and they may have seen power used
destructively by people in authority. Yet women recognize that as they
become successful, they will accrue power which will put them in a
position to affect other people's lives in important ways, such as firing
people, promoting people, and making decisions about how money is used.
Many women are afraid that they will not be liked by others if they are seen
as powerful and as using their power to affect other people's lives. They
have a conflict between their need for power and their need for affiliation
with others. If a person persists in feeling like an impostor, she can imagine
that she is not as powerful as she really is and can thus avoid the negative
consequences she fears.

One of the most useful approaches we have found in helping women
deal with their resistances to giving up impostor feelings is an adaptation of
Aaron Beck's cognitive style of therapy (Beck, Rush, Shaw, & Emery,
1979). First we ask the client to identify what catastrophic thought she is
saying to herself, such as, "If I believed I were intelligent, no one would
like me." Then we ask her to list the advantages and disadvantages of
holding on to that particular thought. Next we have her check the assumed
advantages one by one to see whether they are actually true. One of the
apparent advantages of the catastrophic thought is that the woman is
keeping people from disliking her. In looking at the reality of this belief,
she will likely discover that most people would be happy for her to own her
intelligence, and perhaps a few would feel jealous or threatened. Could she
stand it if a few people felt less than totally positive toward her? When she
has gained more clarity about the specific nature of her fear, she can decide
whether it is truly to her advantage to maintain the belief or not. When we
have guided the client through the entire process of testing the reality of
the assumed advantages as well as listing and confronting all of the disadvantages, she is now in a better position to see more clearly how her
self-concept as an impostor has impeded her and she is more willing to
change her image of herself as an impostor.

Since changing the impostor phenomenon means making a significant identity shift, the therapeutic process is often slow and requires time and patience from therapist and client. However, we have found the therapy process with our high-achieving clients very rewarding. They can and do make changes that have powerful impact on their lives. They spend less and less time and energy negating themselves and gain more enjoyment in the process of achieving and living.

REFERENCES

Ansbacher, H. L., & Ansbacher, R. R. *The individual psychology of Alfred Adler*. New York: Harper Colophon Books, 1956, pp. 172–196.

Beck, A. T., Rush, A. G., Shaw, B. F., & Emery, G. *Cognitive therapy of depression*. New York: Guilford Press, 1979.

Clance, P. R., & Imes, S. A. The impostor phenomenon in high achieving women: Dynamics and therapeutic intervention. *Psychotherapy: Theory, Research and Practice*, 1978, *15*, 241–247.

Harvey, J. C. The impostor phenomenon and achievement: A failure to internalize success. (Doctoral dissertation, Temple University, 1981). *Dissertation Abstracts International*, 1982, 42B, #4969B. (University Microfilm No. A8210500).

Polster, E., & Polster, M. *Gestalt therapy integrated*. New York: Brunner/Mazel, 1973.

Steiner, C. M. *Scripts people live*. New York: Grove Press, 1974.

■ 7

Strategies for Dealing with Sex-role Stereotypes

**IRIS FODOR AND
ESTHER D. ROTHBLUM**

Sex role stereotypes refer to general beliefs about the nature of women and men. When asked to describe typical characteristics of women and men, people tend to describe women as warm and expressive, men as rational and competent (Deaux, 1976). Whereas such personality traits might accurately describe many people, they exclude a significant proportion of the population.

Mental health professionals have not been immune from the use of stereotypes to characterize their clients. In a now-classic study (Broverman, Broverman, Clarkson, Rosenkrantz, & Vogel, 1970), mental health professionals were asked to describe either a healthy man, a healthy woman, or a healthy person. The characteristics used to describe a healthy man and a healthy person were nearly identical, whereas the opposites of these characteristics were used to describe a healthy woman. Thus, it is difficult, even in the eyes of trained professionals, to regard a person as both healthy and female.

A decade later, texts on women in therapy are continuing to report sexist practices by psychologists toward female clients (Howell & Bayes,

1981; Rawlings & Carter, 1977). The themes involving sexism in the Report of the Task Force on Sex Bias and Sex-Role Stereotyping in Psychotherapeutic Practice conducted in 1974 (Brodsky & Holroyd, 1981) include the following: (1) the therapist fostering the traditional sex role, by advocating marriage, housework, or childrearing for women, and deferring to the husband's needs in therapy; (2) devaluation of women via sexist jokes, demeaning comments, or inaccurate labels to describe women; (3) sexist use of pyschodynamic concepts, such as "penis envy," "vaginal orgasm," or "castrating female"; and (4) responding to women as sex objects or seducing female clients.

Similarly, feminist psychopathologists (e.g., Franks & Rothblum, 1983) have stressed the interrelationship between certain types of mental disorders and the feminine sex-role stereotype. As Table 7.1 indicates, classifying DSM III disorders as "male" or "female" as a function of which sex is more prevalent provides a virtual caricature of the male and female sex-role stereotypes; whereas men prevail among the antisocial, "acting-out," "tough" disorders, women are more frequently depressed, anxious, unassertive, and passive.

As societal roles for women are changing and women are struggling to adapt their own history of socialization to the new norms, it is the authors' belief that therapists are increasingly faced with three categories of female clients. First, there are women who seek therapy because they respond to

TABLE 7.1 DSM III Disorders Grouped by Prevalent Sex

Women Predominate	*Men Predominate*
Axis I Disorders	
Depression	Alcoholism
Agoraphobia	Drug abuse
Sexual dysfunction	Antisocial behavior
Simple phobias	Paraphilias
Anxiety states	Transsexualism
Somatization disorder	Factitious disorder
Multiple personality	Pathological gambling
Psychogenic pain disorder	Pyromania
	Intermittent explosive disorder
Axis II Disorders	
Histrionic personality disorder	Paranoid personality disorder
Borderline personality disorder	Antisocial personality disorder
Dependent personality disorder	Compulsive personality disorder

stress with passivity and dependence, as they were socialized only too well to do. Such clients present symptoms of depression, agoraphobia, sexual dysfunction, and anxiety states. Second, clients may seek therapy because they do not fit the feminine stereotype and wish to conform to society's standards of the ideal woman. Thus, women are overrepresented among clients seeking help for being "undesirable" as a result of being "too fat," "unattractive," "too old," or "without a man." They seek help to become more like the stereotype—thinner, attractive, and marriageable. Finally, a third group of clients seeks out therapy in response to the feminist movement and to overcome their original sex-role programming. This group often desires assertion training or coping strategies for the work setting or dealing with untraditional life styles as well as stress management training.

This chapter will discuss each of these categories of female clients by focusing on one representative disorder. Thus, clients presenting symptoms of agoraphobia, obesity, and lack of assertion will be described as they reflect the overly stereotyped woman, the woman wishing to conform more to the stereotype, and the woman wishing to conform less to the stereotype, respectively. The authors are aware that therapists differ in theoretical orientation and are knowledgeable about intervention strategies to decrease the *clinical* symptoms of these disorders. Thus, we will focus only on the components of these disorders that are the result of sex-role socialization. We will similarly provide feminist therapy intervention and prevention strategies for dealing with sex-role stereotypes.

OVERLY STEREOTYPED WOMEN: AGORAPHOBIA

The Broverman et al. (1970) research portrays the healthy woman as emotional, submissive, excitable, passive, home-oriented, tearful, dependent, and not at all adventursome. These terms are equally descriptive of women who come to therapy with phobic disorders. Agoraphobia is the most prevalent phobia and is essentially a female disorder; 85 percent of agoraphobics are women (Fodor, 1982a). In fact, agoraphobics score at the most stereotypically feminine end of the sex-role stereotyping questionnaires (Jassin, 1980). Agoraphobia has often been referred to as the "housebound housewives disorder" due to the high incidence of young married females reporting the syndrome (Brehony, 1983). From clinical discussions several patterns become apparent. The first pattern can be termed the "fear of fear" (Goldstein & Chambless, 1978). This involves worry about the physical symptoms breaking through and leading to panic attacks. The second pattern consists of avoidance behaviors. What agoraphobics fear most are not the feared objects themselves (closed spaces, tunnels), but the trappedness in these situations which relates to anxiety about losing control (becoming hysterical). Agoraphobics similarly fear manifesting the physical symptoms (dizziness, hyperventilation, nausea) with no help or escape possible. A third feature is the lack of development of self-sufficiency. Agoraphobics appear to lack the skills to control themselves when they panic or to function competently in society in an independent way (Fodor, 1974; Goldstein & Chambless, 1978; Marks, 1969, 1970).

Research suggests that a multifaceted feminist approach is the most effective for agoraphobics (Brehony, 1983; Fodor, 1982a; Goldstein & Chambless, 1980). First the socially isolated agoraphobic needs to understand how common agoraphobia is and how many females under pressure feel dependent and helpless. Further, in therapy she can compare aspects of her agoraphobia with the way she was conditioned as a female in our society. Furthermore, the particular pressure in the life of the woman can be explored. She needs validation for how stressful it is to be at home with small children, to be married, and to do the housework; she needs reassurance that it is understandable for her to feel trapped or wish to flee. Finally, we give permission to change. What is the client not doing with her life that she would like to do? In addition to the exposure to the feared situations, she is encouraged to envision other changes, perhaps working outside the home. We also teach self-maintenance strategies so she learns to be less dependent, particularly on her husband. Through all of this the therapist is available as coach, teacher, and role-model. The therapist tries to help the client to view herself as a person in the act of changing.

The two other categories we will discuss are more problematic, since the client needs to work not only on herself, but on the societal appraisal of her behavior.

ATTEMPTING TO CONFORM MORE TO THE STEREOTYPE: OBESITY

Stereotypes about weight in our culture involve the belief that there is an ideal standard of weight for each woman. Hence, according to the Metropolitan Life Insurance Tables, 40 percent of females are classified as more than 20 percent overweight. It is further assumed that obesity is the result of overeating and lack of self-control. Overweight women are considered unattractive and are therefore unlikely to be successful in their pursuit of the societal goals of marriage and material happiness (Fodor, 1982b). Women can be influenced by these stereotypes to the degree that the desire to lose weight becomes a chronic focus of effort and worry with adverse effects on well-being and overall functioning. Wooley and Wooley (1980, p. 137) state:

> The dieting effects . . . may number in the dozens, over spans of 10–40 years and include repeated hospitalizations, stays at reducing spas, multiple forms of hypnotherapies and self-help groups. In its most extreme form, the effort to be slender becomes so central to self-acceptance that all other life activities are relegated to relative unimportance. If weight is too high, the patient will avoid seeing friends, refuse to attend social events, avoid sex and postpone or drop out of training or careers. The plan is always to begin or resume these activities once weight is lost, but for many that day never comes or is short lived.

Women represent over 90 percent of clients at weight-reduction clinics and over 98 percent of clients presenting with bulimia and anorexia. In these disorders, mostly prevalent in adolescents, young women have extremely distorted body images, and some anorexics may starve themselves to emaciation and even death in the belief that they are obese (Fodor, 1982b; Fodor & Thal, 1983).

Feminist therapy for the overweight woman must go beyond assuming that weight reduction is the desired goal. While this past decade has seen a mushrooming of weight-control programs (mostly behavioral), such therapy at best can offer only short-term, minimal weight loss. Typically, a client after repeated battles in weight-reduction programs believes she has two problems: one, that she is overweight and therefore unattractive, and two, that she is a failure because she lacks the necessary self-control to lose weight. Feminist therapy with such clients involves questioning the societally conditioned view of one's body weight.

Clients are given a choice as to whether they wish to focus on weight loss at all or instead to increase self-acceptance of their body. In studying the messages about thin being attractive and fat being unattractive, one needs to point out the recent origins of such messages. In Victorian times, for example, lean was considered repulsive and it was quite desirable for a woman to be voluptuous. Even today, obesity is more medically hazardous for men and more socially hazardous for women (Zegman, 1983). Extreme thinness and physical attractiveness are the norm in the media for success-ful women. Thus, given a lack of overweight role models, clients need to construct their own view of what is desirable and reeducate their social supports. Some women may want to reeducate the media to present normal weight and large women in a multitude of roles.

Finally, in working with weight-reduction clients, the therapist must also get in touch with her own prejudices about body weight and attractive-ness. Fodor and Thal (1983) have reviewed the literature suggesting that helping professionals (particularly physicians) are likely to hold negative attitudes about the obese and to regard them as unattractive and weak-willed. Such stereotypes about obese clients impede clients' self-accep-tance and motivation to change. As Linehan and Egan (1979) have put it, "When half the population is targeted as needing to change their behavior in order to gain fair treatment by the system, we have to ask what system are these individuals trying to fit into." Hopefully, therapy will allow obese women to "fit into" a larger-size society.

ATTEMPTING TO CONFORM LESS TO THE STEREOTYPE: ASSERTION

Nonassertion has been conceptualized as a socially conditioned feminine trait associated with passive, submissive, helpless, and altruistic behaviors in women (Butler, 1976). Assertiveness techniques were developed from work with women in groups to provide an antidote to the traditional feminine nonassertive social programming. Further, feminist therapists hypothesized that women would use assertiveness training to develop their own personal power base in order to confront the male establishment and redress societal inequities (Fodor & Epstein, 1983).

Assertiveness training for women has been immensely popular and has spawned numerous courses, self-help groups, and books. Some of the pioneering integration of feminist therapy with more traditional assertive-ness techniques was done on female assertiveness problems (Jakobowski-Spector, 1973; Wolfe & Fodor, 1975).

Feminist therapy of assertion involves helping women become aware of sex-role socialization messages that contribute to unassertive behavior ("She's such a lovely quiet girl," "Always put other people's feelings first."). Wolfe and Fodor state (1975, p. 45), "It is largely through following out the nurturant, docile programming of the female role . . . denying their own needs, and devoting themselves to winning others' love and approval . . . that women in particular seem to wind up with such severe deficits in assertive behavior." Women are thus encouraged to challenge these beliefs or replace them with more adaptive, assertive, enhancing belief systems that contribute to assertiveness. The therapists and other women in the group serve as models for assertive behavior; thus it is important for the therapist to have appropriate assertive skills.

While the majority of women who have gone through assertiveness training report satisfaction with such training, there exists little research documentation of long-term maintenance (Fodor & Epstein, 1983; String-er-Moore & Jack, 1981). Further, it is in assertiveness training that we are actually demonstrating the conflict over femininity: To be nonassertive is often equated with being feminine and to be assertive is often equated with being masculine. Thus it is difficult to be assertive and still to be perceived as appropriately feminine.

As a consequence, beliefs inhibiting assertive responding may not be so irrational or maladaptive (Fodor, 1980; Linehan & Egan, 1979; Wolfe & Fodor, 1975). Schwartz and Gottman (1976) speak of the deficit in nonassertive persons as the inability to accurately estimate the consequences of their assertions. In women, it may be the *accuracy* of their perception of the consequences that truly inhibits their behavior.

There is now a growing body of research to suggest that there is bias against assertive women (see Solomon and Rothblum, in press, for a review of this literature). It may not be possible for female assertive behaviors to be judged independently of the sex of the participant and observer. Research by Bellack, Hersen, and Turner (1979), among others, suggests that expert judges are influenced by sex of the clients and, in particular, are biased against assertive behavior by women. Rich and Schroeder (1976) report that expert and peer male and female judges both identified comparable noncoercible behaviors when enacted by men as assertive but aggressive when performed by women.

Not only is there bias, but Fiedler and Beach (1978) suggest that behaviors encouraged by assertiveness training often are not rewarded but rather punished. A woman who is learning to be assertive may find that she was more highly valued by her spouse or employer when she was accommodating, self-denying, and passive. Her assertiveness may increase her self-respect, but she may be unwilling to live with the negative reactions of others to her behavior and therefore may cease to use her skills. Thus, to maintain assertive responding and to continue developing an independent stance as a woman in a society that still values female accommodation presents some dilemmas for feminist therapists. We are training our clients to tackle a lonely and difficult path, and we must begin to do research on how to effect change at the societal level, so that the burden of change is not solely on our individual clients. Assertiveness trainers need to work together to develop appropriate techniques to deal with the media and devise programs to effect attitudinal change. We will fail more women unless we can build a better societal reinforcement system.

CONCLUSION

It is evident from the descriptions of disorders affecting women that there are numerous levels of effective intervention. Women need to know that they are not alone in their struggles to cope with changing societal roles. Thus, therapists can serve as role-models or expose clients to similar others as avenues of social support.

Feminist therapists may wish to anticipate clients' needs by serving as educators to society at large. Consulting to schools and advising parents on nonsexist childrearing methods are ways of preventing helpless, passive disorders in girls early on. Feminist therapists can similarly inform colleagues about the influence of stereotypes. Appearances in the media by informed mental health professionals are an excellent way to counter traditional media images of women. Thus, strategies for dealing with sex-role stereotypes need to incorporate prevention as well as intervention methods. Rather than treating the individual client as an isolated case, it is far more cost-effective for feminist therapists to become advocates of a changing society.

REFERENCES

Bellack, A. S., Hersen, M., & Turner, S. Relationship of role playing and knowledge of appropriate behavior to assertion in the natural environment. *Journal of Consulting and Clinical Psychology*, 1979, 47, 670–678.

Brehony, K. A. Women and agoraphobia: A case for the etiological significance of the feminine sex role stereotype. In V. Franks & E. D. Rothblum (Eds.), *The stereotyping of women: The effects on mental health*. New York: Springer, 1983.

Brodsky, A., & Holroyd, J. Report of the task force on sex bias and sex-role stereotyping in psychotherapeutic practice. In E. Howell & M. Bayes (Eds.), *Women and mental health*. New York: Basic Books, 1981.

Broverman, I. K., Broverman, D. M., Clarkson, F. E., Rosenkrantz, P. S., & Vogel, S. R. Sex-role stereotypes and clinical judgments of mental health. *Journal of Consulting and Clinical Psychology*, 1970, *34*, 107.

Butler, P. Assertive training: Teaching women not to discriminate against themselves. *Psychotherapy: Theory, Research and Practice*, 1976, *13*(1), 56–60.

Deaux, K. *The behavior of men and women*. Monterey, Calif.: Brooks/Cole, 1976.

Fiedler, D., & Beach, L. R. On the decision to be assertive. *Journal of Consulting Psychology*, 1978, *46*, 537–546.

Fodor, I. G. The phobic syndrome in women: Implications for treatment. In V. Franks & V. Burtle (Eds.), *Women in therapy*. New York: Brunner/Mazel, 1974.

Fodor, I. G. The treatment of communication problems with assertiveness training. In A. Goldstein & E. Foa (Eds.), *Handbook of behavioral interventions*. New York: Wiley, 1980, 501–603.

Fodor, I. G. Gender and phobia. In Al-Issa Ihsan (Ed.), *Gender and psychopathology*. San Diego, Calif.: Academic Press, 1982. (a)

Fodor, I. G. Behavior therapy for the overweight woman: A time for re-appraisal. In M. Rosenbaum & C. Franks, (Eds.), *Perspectives on behavior therapy in the eighties: Selected and updated proceedings from the First World Congress on Behavior Therapy*. New York: Springer, 1982. (b)

Fodor, I. G., & Epstein, R. Assertiveness training for women: Where are we failing? In P. Emmelkamp & E. Foa (Eds.), *Failures in behavior therapy*. New York: Wiley, 1983.

Fodor, I. G., & Thal, J. The weight disorders—overweight and anorexia: The case for expanded treatment options. In E. Belchman (Ed.), *Behavior modification for women*. New York: Guilford Press, 1983.

Franks, V., & Rothblum, E. D. (Eds.), *The Stereotyping of Women: Its effects on mental health*. New York: Springer Publishing Co., 1983.

Goldstein, A. J., & Chambless, D. L. A reanalysis of agoraphobia. *Behavior Therapy*, 1978, *9*, 47–59.

Goldstein, A. J., & Chambless, D. L. The treatment of agoraphobia. In A. J. Goldstein & E. Foa (Eds.), *Handbook of behavioral interventions*. New York: Wiley, 1980.

Howell, E., & Bayes, M. (Eds.), *Women and mental health*. New York: Basic Books, 1981.

Jakobowski-Spector, P. Facilitating the growth of women through assertive training. *The Counseling Psychologist*, 1973, *4*, 76–86.

Jassin, S. A comparison of agoraphobics, anxiety neurotics, and depressive neurotics using the MMPI and the Beck Depression Inventory. Unpublished dissertation, Temple University, Philadelphia, Penn., 1980.

Linehan, M., & Egan, E. Assertion training for women: Square peg in a round hole? Paper presented at Symposium on Behavior Therapy for Women. Association for the Advancement of Behavior Therapy Annual Meeting, San Francisco, Calif., 1979.

Marks, I. *Fears and phobias*. London: Heinemann, 1969.

Marks, I. Agoraphobic syndrome: Phobic anxiety state. *Archives of General Psychiatry*, 1970, *23*, 538–553.

Rawlings, E. I., & Carter, D. K. *Psychotherapy for women: Treatment toward equality*. Springfield, Ill.: Charles C. Thomas, 1977.

Rich, A. R., & Schroeder, H. E. Research issues in assertiveness training. *Psychological Bulletin*, 1976, *83*, 1081–1096.

Schwartz, R. M., & Gottman, J. M. Toward a task analysis of assertive behavior. *Journal of Consulting and Clinical Psychology*, 1976, *44*, 910–920.

Solomon, L. J., & Rothblum, E. D. Social skills problems experienced by women. In L. L'Abate & M. P. Milan (Eds.), *Handbook of social skills training and research*. New York: Wiley, in press.

Stringer-Moore, D., & Jack, G. B. *Assertive behavior training: A cross-referenced annotated bibliography*. San Luis Obispo: Impact, 1981.

Wolfe, J. L., & Fodor, I. G. A cognitive behavioral approach to modifying assertive behavior in women. *The Counseling Psychologist*, 1975, *5*, 45–52.

Wooley, S. C., & Wooley, O. W. Women and weight: Toward a redefinition of the therapeutic task. In A. Brodsky & R. Hare-Mustin (Eds.), *Women and psychotherapy: An assessment of research and practice*. New York: Guilford Press, 1980.

Zegman, M. A. Women, weight, and health. In V. Franks & E. D. Rothblum (Eds.), *The stereotyping of women: Its effects on mental health*. New York: Springer, 1983.

■8

Psychotherapy of Black Women and the Dual Effects of Racism and Sexism

FRANCES K. TROTMAN

SOME ORIGINS OF THE IMPOSTER PHENOMENON AMONG BLACK WOMEN

Black women have experienced the imposter phenomenon, i.e., an internal experience of intellectual phoniness (Clance & Imes, 1978) by virtue of being both black people in white America and women in a male-dominated culture. Indeed, "black women have been doubly victimized by scholarly neglect and racist assumptions. Belonging as they do to two groups which have traditionally been treated as inferiors by American society—blacks and women—they have been doubly invisible." (Lerner, 1973, p. xvii).

Women and blacks are neither noted nor valued for their academic achievements or intellectual contributions to our culture. Growing up black in America, one is constantly struck with negative references associ-

96

ated with being black. Since the earliest days of slavery, racist practices and ideology, extending beyond the individual behavior of white persons into the institutional structure and cultural mores of the United States, have had as their goal the dehumanization of black people (Kovel, 1970). "Dehumanization involves first forming an idea of another living person as a 'thing' so as to sustain one's dehumanized conception of [her]" (Kovel, 1970, p. 36).

Oppressive, racist America, with its implication to the black child that she could never be, have, or achieve as much as a white person, certainly affects the black woman's perception of herself. Oppressive experiences associated with being black together with America's idea of a woman's role could very well leave the black woman with an at least subliminal image of herself as a dumb, lazy, shiftless, baby-producing housewife with perhaps a lot of rhythm, but not much else.

In a culture which dictates that success and intellectual achievement are not the domain of such a person, the black woman is hard-pressed to believe in her own capabilities. One's self-concept must be affected and self-esteem is likely to suffer as a result of such damaging appraisals by the society into which the black girl child is born.

Research concerning the self-esteem of black Americans has not been conclusive. "Both the lack of specificity of a test and the situational quality of self-esteem may be reflected in the contradictory literature on self-esteem of black children" (Jenkins, 1982, p. 29). However, when black children have been requested to express a preference for dolls (Clark & Clark, 1952; Porter, 1971), or pictures (Williams & Morland, 1976), or of lighter as opposed to darker people or animals, they tend to choose the lighter ones (McAdoo, 1977). (For an exhaustive review of self-concept and self-esteem studies, see Gordon, 1977).

Yet the individual may choose from among a number of characteristics in her efforts to maintain self-esteem. "One's self-esteem may be based upon such varied characteristics as athletic prowess, dress and physical appearance, attractiveness to the opposite sex, skill at verbal repartee and skill at fighting, as well as academic achievement" (Epps, 1975, p. 305); and black and white persons probably value some components of self-concept differently (Baldwin, 1979).

Indeed, despite the overwhelming oppressiveness of growing up a black and a woman in America, the black American woman has somehow survived. "As we look at the history of blacks, we find that they have responded to the situations they confronted with an underlying premise of self-worth and competence even though external circumstances did not seem to warrant positive self-appraisals" (Jenkins, 1982, p. 19).

Perhaps African social practices that distributed tribal authority among women as well as men (see Carey, 1979) helped to counteract for black women some of the historical oppression of American women. A distinctive element in the experience of black women is the relative lack among black people of a strong patriarchal tradition characteristic of the white culture (Yorburg, 1974). The black woman has often been the sole economic support of her family. And as doors open to the educated black women, one might expect them to have fewer conflicts about aspiration and achievement.

Another consideration adding to the complexity of the "imposter" status of the black woman is the role of the black male and particularly the black woman's response and reactions to him and his position in America. Michelle Wallace (1980) feels that the black woman's plight has been further aggravated by her subordination to the black male. On the other hand, the sentiments expressed by Dara Abubakari (see Lerner, 1973) in the following passage take a different view and are seen by Wallace (1980) as a further means of subjugating black women and denying their person-hood:

> The role of black women at this point in history is to give sustenance to the black man. At one time the black woman was the only one that could say something and not get her head chopped off. . . . But the law was strictly against the black man. So he could not do anything. Now that he speaks, we speak together. We cannot separate, and this is what I say to the women's lib movement. . . . The black woman is not undergoing the same kind of oppression that white women have gone through in the home. The black woman is liberated in her own mind, because she has taken on the responsibil-ity for the family and she works. Black women had to get in the labor force, because black men didn't have jobs.
>
> The point is that . . . the struggle of black women and white women is not the same. Because the white woman is oppressed and is only now realizing her oppression. White women, middle-class women, have to look at their prob-lem and it is their husbands. He is the oppressor, because he is the system. It's a white male system (Lerner, 1973, pp. 585–586).

Whether or not the black woman's relationship with the black man represents either support or subordination is indicative of the complexity of forces tugging on the allegiance of black women. A whole range of intense sentiments such as those of Wallace on the one hand and Abubakari on the other can be found among the black female population.

Surely the antecedents and components of the imposter phenomenon for black women are different and perhaps more complex than those which help to account for the phenomenon among white women. Being born both a black person and a woman in twentieth-century America represents a double attack on one's self-image, whereas, on the other hand, black history and African social practices (see Carey, 1979) may have afforded black women some degree of authority and feelings of self-worth.

To further complicate matters are the effects of skin color, social class, and environment on the black woman and her perception of who she is in America. Varieties of skin color, and variations in living style from Bedford-Stuyvesant to Beverly Hills, serve to further complicate the psychology as well as the implications for psychotherapeutic intervention in the life of the black woman. The concept of herself as a black person and the concomitant implications may be very different for the light-skinned, upper-class black raised in Scarsdale or Beverly Hills than for her dark-skinned lower-class sister from Bedford-Stuyvesant or Watts.

It has been my observation, however, that the shorter the length of time that the achieving black woman's family has been in the middle class, the more likely she is to feel the effects of the imposter phenomenon. Because of slavery and its legacy of oppression, most black families are very new entrants to middle-class life and the imposter phenomenon is, therefore, widespread and thriving among achieving middle-class black women.

It is the first-generation middle-class achieving black woman who has perhaps recently learned to suppress or mask her rage (see Grier & Cobbs, 1968) or feeling of inadequacy or sense of degradation enough to "fool" others into believing that she really belongs. And like any victim of the imposter phenomenon, she is in constant fear of detection. It is such a woman who is likely to present herself to a psychotherapist with vague feelings of insecurity, depression, or anxiety which seem incomprehensible to her in view of her "unusual" successes.

Because the antecedents and components of the imposter phenomenon are different for black women than for white women, it is crucial that the therapist for the achieving black woman be intimately aware of black culture. It is critical that the black woman suffering the imposter phenomenon feels safe enough and understood enough to share her feelings of fraudulence. A group experience with other achieving black women who risk exploring the commonality of fraudulent feelings is particularly therapeutic in such cases.

FEMINIST PSYCHOTHERAPY AND THE BLACK WOMAN

Issues in the psychotherapy of black women are crucial, significant, and often controversial. As black women increasingly seek professional consultation for emotional difficulties, it is imperative that we evaluate existing approaches, particularly feminist approaches, for their relevance to the black female experience. In examining the appropriateness of specific therapeutic interventions for black women, several issues must be considered. Among the most salient are (1) the race of the therapist, (2) the importance of the culture and social class of the therapist, (3) the effect of therapists' attitudes, (4) the same sex versus the opposite sex therapist, and (5) the importance of role-modeling. As director of a psychotherapy institute in a socioeconomically and ethnically heterogeneous area, I have the responsibility of ensuring an appropriate match between therapist and client in order to maximize the therapeutic potential of the dyad.

For the black female client, an obvious consideration is the race of the therapist. It is understandable that the black client will bring her preconceptions and perhaps strong feelings concerning the race of her therapist. She might, for example, see the white therapist as representative of authority, more concerned about justifying society's positions than in empathically relating to the client and her problems. In considering the race of the therapist for the black woman, my decisions have been influenced by my experiences and observations, a great deal of literature, and some research. In general, the black therapist is less likely to be seduced or manipulated by the black female client who has learned to use her blackness as a weapon to maintain power or to punish others by eliciting compassion or guilt; because of his or her own feelings, the white therapist is reluctant to suggest to the client her responsibility for her own life.

Other behaviors which are more readily seen in the white therapist/ black client relationship are the therapist as the self-appointed advocate, as the client controller, or as self-effacing and therefore neither genuine nor completely available to the client. As the self-appointed advocate and as the client controller, the therapist assumes undue responsibility for the client and in his or her paternalism implies an inequality in their humanity and a disrespect for the client's judgment and abilities. Many well-meaning, dedicated, and sympathetic white therapists are often trapped by the symbolism of their white skin in view of Afro-American history and the subtle pervasiveness of America's guilt.

In the relationship between the black therapist and the black woman, there are other potential dangers. There is the possibility that the black therapist will become overidentified with the client as a victim of the system and aid her in denial of responsibility for her life. Some of this behavior might enhance the relationship through a feeling of sisterhood. As we all know, however, it is extremely important that the client develop a sense of responsibility for her own life despite any obstacles imposed by her ethnicity.

Another danger for the black therapist (and occasionally the white therapist) is that he or she will attempt to raise the consciousness of any black woman who is seemingly unaware of the circumstances, history, and implications of her blackness. Such interventions may be quite instructional and educational. They are not, however, always therapeutic and often lead to premature termination by a client who may be either uninterested in or defended against such information.

At the other end of the spectrum is the black therapist who has dissociated his or her self from his or her blackness, harboring a core of self-hatred and rejection of anything reminiscent of the black culture. Such a therapist poses the danger of engendering feelings of rejection and self-hatred in the black female client, thereby creating a relationship which is not only not therapeutic, but often detrimental.

On the other hand, there are many advantages of a black therapist/black female client alliance. Most black therapists are aware of those types of black women's behaviors that are different from the white norm and might be considered pathological by someone unfamiliar with the black culture, e.g., distrust of police or authority figures may be seen as pathological when it is in fact justified by the reality of corrupt ghetto policemen or other authority figures who may abuse their power in the black community. Often patients are diagnosed as more severely disturbed by a white therapist than they would be by a black therapist (Lerner, 1972). Often nonnormative behaviors are appropriate and functional for black women but less readily comprehensible to the white therapist, e.g., belief in spiritualism or "readers and advisors" may be seen as pathological by someone unfamiliar with the black culture. Also the black therapist is frequently more likely to realize that traditional interventions and the 50-minute hour are often less effective for the black female, who may require active intervention and assistance with such things as housing or discrimination before she can attend to her intra-psychic conflicts.

Furthermore, knowing what a clients's words might refer to symbolically in her experience obviously makes it more possible to translate thoughts and feelings in order to reveal more of what the self is about. The ability to make these kinds of translations is essential to dynamic therapies (Edelson, 1975).

There has been some interesting research in this area concerning race of the therapist for the black client in general that is likely to be applicable to the black woman in particular. Turner and Armstrong (1981) found that white therapists do not experience racial issues in psychotherapy with the same salience as black therapists, yet they report higher levels of subjective distress in cross-cultural treatment. The white therapists' distress focused on "negative attitudes" of clients, therapists' feelings of not being able to help or to confront different race clients, or being oversolicitous or too distant with different race clients. Research on psychotherapy with blacks suggests that "the nature and quality of therapist–patient interaction is a critical determinant in whether a black client continues psychotherapy" (Griffith & Jones, 1979, p. 229). A number of studies indicate that blacks drop out of therapy at a high rate quite early (see, for example, Sue, McKinney, Allen, & Hall, 1974; Sue, 1977). Some research has found that "depth of self-exploration" in black clients was enhanced when those clients were seen by black interviewers (Banks, 1972; Carkhuff & Pierce, 1967). Griffith and Jones (1979) report a number of other similar studies in which clients expressed preference for black counselors or felt better understood by them. (These were, however, "analogue" studies.) Sattler (1970) cites studies of assessment, interview, educational, and therapeutic situations to show an inhibiting effect on the black client when the authority is white.

Black patients from neurotic, middle-class populations, however, have been shown to profit in cross-racial therapies (Jones, 1978). In the Jones studies there was the opportunity to compare outcome and details of therapy process in the four kinds of black-white/therapist-client matches. No differences were found in overall outcome—as a group, clients in all the different therapies got better to about the same degree, as far as the measures used could tell. There were differences by racial match-up, however, in the process of the therapy relationships, that is, in the nature of the interpersonal dynamics that occurred between therapist and client.

Addressing the white therapist/black client relationship, Griffith and Jones (1979) note:

> The race difference appears to have its greatest impact early in treatment, particularly at the first encounter. If the white therapist can establish effective rapport at initial contact and build a therapeutic alliance in relatively rapid fashion, successful outcomes can be achieved with lower income black clients despite their initial sense of wariness and consequently slower movement in therapy (p. 230).

It has indeed been my experience and observation that black women depend more on their initial affective assessment of the therapeutic situation than on any objective criteria over time. For the black woman entering therapy, the therapeutic alliance may automatically conjure up the spectre of an authoritarian institution operating on the potential client to her detriment. The history of psychiatric treatment of blacks in America does not refute this (Thomas & Sillen, 1972; Willie, Kramer, & Brown, 1973). Also, professional consultation for psychological difficulties is not something that springs naturally from the black woman's experience. She is understandably wary, and the cultural unfamiliarity may heighten her tendency to rely more on affective assessments as a way of judging whether or not this is going to be a useful experience. This may mean that a potential client may be particularly sensitive to the initial difficulties that are bound to occur between strangers, particularly from different cultural backgrounds. (I will speak more about dealing with those issues later in this chapter.)

There are additional therapeutic considerations for the black woman which are more specifically cultural or attitudinal than purely racial. Tomes (1976) cites various recent studies indicating differential attitudes toward blacks who present themselves for treatment. The tendency to see blacks as too sick or inappropriate for talking therapies or not really psychologically disturbed may be a way of "avoiding their own race and class attitudes on the part of the white professional" and also of avoiding "exposure to the intense feelings that black clients may want to vent . . . concerning their social and racial as well as their personal concerns" (Jenkins, 1982, p. 155). Many black women are very sensitive to any indication on the part of the therapist that she may be masking or avoiding her own difficulties through quick preconceptions of blacks and hasty, inaccurate interpretations. This is obviously detrimental to the therapeutic process, particularly if it is kept undercover and unexpressed.

It is generally recognized now that verbalness depends on the situation in which people find themselves (Labov, 1972; Lerner, 1972). When lower-class Afro-Americans feel comfortable and understood, they are quite expressive and reflective. The black woman may have traditional reservations concerning immediate trust and self-disclosure; the guilt feelings and anxiety of the therapist can cause the client to further strengthen her defense against intimacy.

Dealing with black rage (Grier & Cobbs, 1968) is often both central and crucial to therapy with Afro-Americans. The experience of self-hatred and degradation imposed on black people in America have left psychic wounds and scars which cannot be left unattended if psychological health is to be realized. Such experiences as the subtle but perhaps devastating feeling among blacks concerning gradations of skin color and hair texture, or the childhood memories of being the darkest or lightest member of the family or community, are often difficult or impossible for the black client to express to her white therapist. Yet these are often the very issues which cause the greatest pain and destruction, particularly if left unexplored.

Along with the experience of anger and rage, a widespread feeling of sadness, a kind of "cultural depression," is part of the black individual's response to historical and current conditions in America (Comer, 1972; Grier & Cobbs, 1968; Poussaint, 1972). It is essential for the therapist of the black woman to understand and ideally to have felt these feelings in order to facilitate the therapeutic process for the black woman.

Black rage and "cultural depression" are certainly not the sole predispositions that are likely to be brought into therapy by the black woman. Block (1981) suggests that "the black culture stresses early in life the ability to 'do it.' Emphasis is placed on the active—managing difficult situations without showing stress" (p. 179). There are many such cultural tendencies which must be understood and preferably experienced by the therapist in order to completely "be with" the black female client. Whenever therapists have experienced situations and feelings similar to those of their clients or patients, there is the greater likelihood of communications of empathy and understanding—not only mutual trust, but a deeper experience of kinship.

Along these same lines are considerations concerning sex of the therapist for the black woman (certainly an appropriate consideration for this volume). It would surely seem that

> by virtue of having a female body and the opportunity to have played the roles of girl baby, daughter, sister, wife, lover, pregnant woman, mother, divorcee,

widow, and grandmother, a woman does have unique experiences, different from men, that she may find especially useful in understanding her women patients, and from which patients may profit (Goz, 1981, p. 516).

The apparent simplicity of this is somewhat complicated, however, by the Porché and Banikotes (1982) findings that white female counselors were perceived as more expert than their black female counterparts, whereas the higher rating of male counselors was not influenced by the racial variable for black adolescents. These findings might seem to indicate that the woman therapist and the black female therapist in particular would have difficulty treating the black woman because of the clients' low expectations and lack of respect for the "expertness" of the black female therapist.

Given America's view of blacks and of women, these findings are quite understandable and do not, in fact, present the problems that they appear to. Phyllis Chesler (1975) has noted that women in the past have preferred male therapists because they mistrusted women as both authorities and people. Similarly, black female adolescents have internalized society's view of black women as not as "expert" as white men. The question is, however, how much the aura of "expert" achieves in the therapeutic relationship. It does not, as one might think, get black women to prefer white males to black females as therapists. It has certainly been my experience that black women overwhelmingly prefer a black woman to a white man as a therapist. Once in the therapist's office, the aura of "expert" may give the therapist more power to use persuasion and suggestion but may actually hinder efforts to create an atmosphere of warmth, empathy, genuineness, and unconditional positive regard.

Though she may not be initially perceived as "expert" by her black female client, the black female therapist serves an important function as a role model for the black woman in treatment. As she communicates honesty, sincerity, and love to her black clients, the black therapist subtly and simultaneously also identifies the details and mechanisms of her own success, thereby demystifying success and making it more accessible to the black female client. In her authenticity, the therapist may relinquish the power and awe of her "expert" or superwoman status for the satisfaction of facilitating the possibility of duplication of her own success for her client.

This brings us to the actual conduct of the therapeutic relationship with the black woman. As can be inferred from the above, many of the elements and practices of what has been referred to in this book as "feminist psychotherapy" are very effective with the black populations. A reduction of the traditional distance between therapist and client encourages the black woman to take control of her life rather than rely on the omniscient "master" who directs her behavior. A lifelong encouragement of black dependency is subtly redirected by the "feminist" psychotherapeutic relationship and the embodiment of egalitarianism.

There are some obvious differences in the "feminist" psychotherapy of black women versus white women. In raising the woman's consciousness to the cultural impact on her growth, for example, both the culture and its impact will differ between the races. The cultures' view of what is "pretty," "sexy," "masculine," or "independent" may touch a black woman's life very differently. Black women have historically been defined as "not" pretty, perhaps "too" sexy, too independent, and "castrating matriarchs"—taking over her man's role when she was forced to support her family. These and other differences change the cultural context in which therapy must take place for the black woman. It is imperative therefore, as suggested above, that the therapist be intimately acquainted with the black woman's culture.

Keeping the above-mentioned cautions in mind, it is the behaviors involved in feminist psychotherapy with the basic tenets of modeling an egalitarian relationship, authenticity, and encouragement of the client's responsibility for her own life that are most likely to facilitate the black woman's escape from the psychological chains and weights imposed by over 300 years of oppression. Therapeutic interventions which embody these traits as opposed to traditional authoritarian approaches seem most effective in facilitating the quickest expression and release from the feelings of phoniness and fraud for the black client. Honesty, sincerity, openness, and risk-taking behavior on the part of the therapist can serve to help other women and blacks to more fully and self-confidently realize their own human potential despite any perceived dictates of society.

REFERENCES

Baldwin, J. A. Theory and research concerning the notion of black self-hatred: A review and reinterpretation. *Journal of Black Psychology*, 1979, 5, 51–78.

Banks, W. M. The differential effect of race and social class in helping. *Journal of Clinical Psychology*, 1972, 28, 90–92.

Block, C. B. Black Americans and the cross-cultural counseling and psychotherapy experience. In A. J. Marsella & P. B. Pedersen (Eds.), *Cross-cultural counseling and psychotherapy*. Elmsford, N.Y.: Pergamon Press, 1981.

Carey, P. M. Black women—a perspective. *Tenth-Year Anniversary Commemorative Monograph Series*, Vol. 1, No. 3. New York: New York University, Institute for Afro-American Affairs, May 1979.

Carkhuff, R. R., & Pierce, R. Differential effects of therapist race and social class upon patient depths of self-exploration in the initial clinical interview. *Journal of Consulting Psychology*, 1967, *31*, 632–634.

Chesler, P. Women as psychiatric and psychotherapeutic patients. In R. K. Unger & F. L. Denmark (Eds.), *Woman—Dependent or Independent Variable?* New York: Psychological Dimensions, 1975, pp. 137–162.

Clance, P. R., & Imes, S. A. The imposter phenomenon in high achieving women: Dynamics and therapeutic interventions. *Psychotherapy: Theory, Research and Practice*, 1978, *15*, pp. 241–247.

Clark, K. B., & Clark, M. P. Racial identification and preference in Negro children. In G. E. Swanson, T. M. Newcomb, & E. L. Hartley (Eds.), *Readings in social psychology*. (Rev. ed.). New York: Holt, Rinehart & Winston, 1952.

Comer, J. P. *Beyond black and white*. New York: Quadrangle, 1972.

Edelson, M. *Language and interpretation in psychoanalysis*. New Haven: Yale University Press, 1975.

Epps, E. G. The impact of school desegregation on aspirations, self-concepts and other aspects of personality. *Law & Contemporary Problems*, 1975, *39*, 300–313.

Gordon, V. V. *The self-concept of black Americans*. Washington, D.C.: University Press of America, 1977.

Goz, R. Women patients and women therapists; Some issues that come up in psychotherapy. In E. Howell & M. Bayes (Eds.), *Women and Mental Health*. New York: Basic Books, 1981.

Grier, W. H., & Cobbs, P. M. *Black rage*. New York: Basic Books, 1968.

Griffith, M. S., & Jones, E. E. Race and psychotherapy: Changing perspectives. In J. H. Masserman (Ed.), *Current psychiatric therapies* (Vol. 18). New York: Grune & Stratton, 1979.

Jenkins, A. H. *The psychology of the Afro-American: A humanistic approach*. New York: Pergamon, 1982.

Jones, E. E. Effects of race on psychotherapy process and outcome: An exploratory investigation. *Psychotherapy: Theory, Research and Practice*, 1978, *15*, 226–236.

Kovel, J. *White racism: A psychohistory*. New York: Pantheon Books, 1970.

Labov, W. Language in the inner city: *Studies in the black English vernacular*. Philadelphia: University of Pennsylvania Press, 1972.

Lerner, B. *Therapy in the ghetto: Political impotence and personal disintegration*. Baltimore: Johns Hopkins University Press, 1972.

Lerner, G. (Ed.) *Black women in white America: A documentary history*. New York: Vintage, 1973.

McAdoo, H. P. The development of self-concept and race attitudes in black children: A longitudinal study. In W. E. Cross, Jr. (Ed.), *Proceedings: The third annual conference on empirical research in black psychology*. Washington, D. C.: U.S. Department of Health, Education, & Welfare, National Institute of Education, 1977.

Porché, L. M., & Banikotes, P. G. Racial and attitudinal factors affecting the perceptions of counselors of black adolescents. *Journal of Counseling Psychology*, March 1982, 29 (2), 169–174.

Porter, J. D. R. *Black child, white child: The development of racial attitudes*. Cambridge: Harvard University Press, 1971.

Poussaint, A. F. *Why blacks kill blacks*. New York: Emerson Hall, 1972.

Sattler, J. Racial "experimenter effects" in experimentation, testing, interviewing, and psychotherapy. *Psychological Bulletin*, 1970, 73, 137–160.

Sue, S., McKinney, H., Allen, D., & Hall, J. Delivery of community mental health services to black and white clients. *Journal of Consulting and Clinical Psychology*, 1974, 42, 794–801.

Sue, S. Community mental health services to minority groups: Some optimism, some pessimism. *American Psychologist*, 1977, 32, 616–624.

Thomas, A., & Sillen, S. *Racism and psychiatry*. New York: Brunner/Mazel, 1972.

Tomes, H. The impact of cultural influences on psychotherapy. In J. L. Claghorn (Ed.), *Successful psychotherapy*. New York: Brunner/Mazel, 1976.

Turner, S., & Armstrong, S. A. Cross-racial psychotherapy: What the therapists say. *Psychotherapy: Theory, Research and Practice*, Fall 1981, 18 (3), 375–378.

Wallace, M. *Black macho and the myth of the superwoman*. New York: Women Books, 1980.

Williams, J. E., & Morland, J. K. *Race, color, and the young child*. Chapel Hill: University of North Carolina Press, 1976.

Willie, C. V., Kramer, B. M., & Brown, B. S. (Eds.). *Racism and mental health*. Pittsburgh: University of Pittsburgh Press, 1973.

Yorburg, B. *Sexual identity: Sex roles and social change*. New York: Wiley, 1974.

■9

Feminist Therapy with Minority Clients[1]

CLAIRE M. BRODY

PSYCHOTHERAPY AND CULTURAL SIMILARITY

There is a small body of literature and a great deal of myth about the advantage of psychotherapy in a context of cultural similarity. Although some research verifies that psychotherapists have been least effective with poor populations in the past, there are many causal variables that have not always been well-controlled in the experimental studies. Bell (1971) points out that most counseling psychologists, black or white, have been through training programs where special needs, values, and life experiences of minorities are ignored. The best that can be hoped for is that an inexperienced therapist can get a chance to focus on her own growth potential. Bell clearly states that no amount of theoretical insight, technical competence, or information about blacks can ensure that a therapist—black or white—can function effectively in the black community; it is the personal impact of

---

1. This paper was the basis for a Conversation Hour, "The Politics of Psychotherapy with Minorities," with Frances K. Trotman at the American Psychological Association Annual Meeting, Washington, D.C., August, 1982.

the therapist on the client that determines the client's receptivity to change.

Sattler (1977), providing an exceptionally fine review of the literature on a broad spectrum of therapeutic issues relating to white therapists working with black clients, concludes, that while there may be black clients who can work successfully only with black therapists, this does not apply to every black client; being a black or white therapist does not automatically guarantee either success or failure. Rather, in interracial therapy this is dependent on many variables, including competence and sensitivity. I was impressed by the remarks of an Hispanic therapist who worked largely with cultural peers. He said, "There is no formula for achieving intimacy. The client cannot always share just because we shared a common cultural heritage."[2]

Recent studies by Turner and Armstrong (1981) and Jones and Seagull (1977) point to interesting differences between black and white therapists in their respective perceptions of the successfulness of cross-racial therapy. These authors say that a client's membership in a lower socioeconomic and minority ethnic group has the potential for being a negative factor in the therapy process. (It is to be noted that no distinction is made for those clients who may be a member of *one* of the foregoing, but not necessarily the other group at the same time.) These writers also emphasize that those two variables are more important as a cause for dropping out of therapy prematurely than color differences between the client and therapist. Vontress (1969), enumerating significant factors in success or lack of it in cross-racial therapy, pointed to some combination of the client's and counselor's reciprocal racial attitudes: the language barrier of poor people generally and of Hispanics in particular (note that here no distinction is made between the possible differences in language facility of "Hispanics," depending on their national origin and educational backgrounds); the client's lack of familiarity with counseling as an avenue of change; the black's traditional reservation about self-disclosure; and leftover sex and race taboos. Aside from the inherent stereotyping in these ascribed traits, I would say that success is more related to characterological variables, and cultural background—not color—of therapist and client.

2. John Munoz at New York Society of Clinical Psychologists Symposium, December 16, 1978. Topic: Cultural-Ethnic Factors in the Treatment of Minority Populations.

In my work with clients who are culturally different from me, I have learned that one characterological variable of the therapist that *can* intrude on the treatment process is guilt. No one is totally free of the remnants of prejudice at some level of awareness. Especially when it is conscious, it can result in guilt, and this in turn can lead to anxiety in the therapist, and cause a client to strengthen her defenses against intimacy and trust. If, as a result of this anxiety, I try too hard, a client has less freedom in choosing or not choosing to respond to my effort to help. If I become frustrated, even angry at the client's intransigence, the client's progress is hindered. The client may need to hold on to the feeling that I am simply a repeat of previously rejecting significant others. I may react defensively and misperceive a client's rage as personal rejection—and thus discourage the client's real need to vent her anger. It is hard to side-step defensiveness under this kind of attack. With all women clients, whether culturally similar or different, I am often thwarted in my attempts to help them feel equal; for clients who are both female and from a minority group, there is still an implicit barrier to feeling equal with someone representing a group they may have been conditioned to mistrust.

THE ISSUE OF TRUST
IN THERAPY WITH MINORITIES

My own experiences with black women in treatment have borne out some but not all of the early predictions that are referred to by Wolken, Morwaki, and Williams (1973). These writers stated that self-disclosure and attitude toward psychotherapy are strongly correlated with similarity of social class of client and therapist; similarity of race was much less significant in this regard. In my practice, when the clients were middle-class black women and I could share values and work histories that included discrimination experiences, the strong bond which resulted transcended color differences. The establishment of mutual trust was undoubtedly the crucial issue, as these authors also pointed out. With acknowledgment that selection factors may have been at work, I have rarely found racial disparity to be a bar to success in treatment *once the women decided to work with me*. I will elaborate some possible reasons for these successes.

One of the main aids for dealing with the trust issue has been for me to offer black women a concomitant group experience. In a mixed racial group, black women have been forced to deal with their fears and distortions about acceptance, with less possibility of escaping or denying their own responsibility for negative responses. Multiple mirrors are a good antidote for distorted perception. Success and failure in the groups appear to have hinged more on the many subtle personal identification factors and the client's particular characterological makeup than on color or ethnic differences.

In the groups of women that were homogeneous in regard to socioeconomic and educational level but racially heterogeneous, most of the women were self-referred. A few came through community agencies but were self-motivated to remain in treatment once they began. The black women came to treatment for basically the same reasons as the white women in my practice. I have found that in putting together a small group (six women seems an ideal size), having a wide age range has also helped: one or two women in their late 40s or 50s lent further diversity to the experience of younger minority women who might be anxious about their ethnic or racial difference and translate this anxiety into mistrust generally.

The evidence from my work with minority women clients supports the view that a woman therapist can produce a positive impetus for trust and change. I am reminded of a young female Moslem student who had struggled with traditional sex discrimination in her family and societal milieu from early childhood. In the American university setting, her conflicts over sex role, sexual behavior, and acceptance were enormous. Her upbringing could not have been more different from my own. Our value systems found a meeting ground when I could empathize with her wish to achieve a totally different woman's role from the one she had been socialized to expect. When she learned to trust me, her severe panic and distortions of reality lessened and she was able to begin to work on her severely damaged self-concept.

In contrast, when treating several Jamaican males at a university counseling center, there was a pattern of chauvinism in sex roles, perpetuated for them throughout childhood and young adulthood, that was now projected onto me, a woman therapist. This was a block to acceptance of help from an (unconsciously) perceived inferior person, and no trust developed. Similarly, one black woman with whom I worked needed to remind me repeatedly that I could not possibly understand her problems of trust, her need for independence, her need to control others, and so on, since I had not grown up in the black ghetto poverty that she had. A poor

Jewish ghetto, she would remind me, had no resemblance whatsoever to the one she had known.

Nevertheless, I probably have been as successful as I have in treating clients different from me because I have been perceived as basically accepting of cultural, class, and color differences; at the same time, I have not been too inhibited by guilt to seem to need to make reparations.

THE POLITICAL REALITY
FOR MINORITY WOMEN

When a female therapist focuses on helping a woman function autonomously, she is limited by what the woman has experienced in the past as a "facilitating environment." ("Facilitating environment" is a term taken over by Vanderson [1974] from Donald Winnicott.) The significant components are the quality of the parenting she received that enabled her to feel like a cherished child; the encouragement for and the tolerance of her increasing autonomy and individuality as she grew; and the availability of appropriate models for identification. These factors might be more significant for a black child, who has even more need for positive reinforcement for being "good" and valued. The burden of functioning in a nonfacilitating environment, from childhood on, is what characterizes the largest proportion of my clientele.

I treated one black woman who was the youngest of three sisters, with about 15 years between her and the next older one. She grew up largely as an "only" child, one cherished by parents who, by that time, were also in a better economic position and could ensure that she had more education than the others. Having grown up on an isolated farm, her adult problems stemmed from having had few peers for friendship available in her preadolescent years and few adult models for achievement-goal identification. There was also little tolerance in her more elderly parents for her growing autonomy and individuality. In several other black women where there was much less of a "facilitating environment"—a one-parent family or economic hardship—there seemed to be more angry determination to be "good," to make a personal statement of worth, at any cost. These women were more available in their therapy for remodeling an achieving self-image. I have had more success with them, perhaps because I was the first significant other who *expected* them to achieve and encouraged this. The black woman from the more facilitating early environment was comparable to an overprotected white child whose adolescent drives are more focused on acquiring independence than becoming successful.

In 1974 Horner and Walsh reminded us that women still tended to view competition, independence, intellectual achievement, and leadership as basically in conflict with femininity, and they paid a high toll for defiance of sex roles. Horner and Walsh also pointed out that while this was true for white women, it was less so for black women; among black women, independence and successful accomplishments were not as incompatible with being a woman. This is still true today; however, there is some difference of opinion as to whether black women, as they rise in the achievement scale, will modify their behavior and internalize the same types of barriers to success that white women did earlier as they stepped out of traditional roles. Horner and Walsh pointed out that there is still a complex relationship between a woman's personality and disposition, based on an array of developmental variables and situational factors, which in turn determine the nature of the expected consequences. This view, modified by King (1973), adamantly differentiates the kind of sexual discrimination and stereotyping that black women experience as compared to white women. She focuses on the race and class variety of stereotypes, rather than just the sexual ones. These stereotypes serve to exacerbate the problems of black women whose development is still a function of the caste system in this country, fraught with myths and images that affect the politics of their functioning in society.

In feminist therapy, a woman client—black or white—does not need to ask as often as she did when she was treated by a male therapist, how free from the dictates of a sexist society she can be. She also no longer has to settle for a female therapist who is male-oriented, sometimes as much a sexist as her male counterpart. I agree with Lerman (1978) that there are undoubtedly a small number of male therapists today who operate in a manner that is parallel to the mode adopted by many female therapists. A study by Sherman, Koufacos, and Kenworthy (1978), however, showed that sex bias and sex-role stereotyping are not uncommon in psychotherapeutic practice, but that they are more common with male than female therapists. They showed that male therapists were less well informed about women's attitudes on key feminine issues. Ensuring an egalitarian, authentic relationship, even with the difficulties it presents for both the client and the therapist, may be the most significant contribution feminist therapists offer minorities.

REFERENCES

Bell, R. L. The culturally deprived psychologist. *Counseling Psychology*, 1971, *2* (4), 104–106.

Horner, M., & Walsh, M. R. Psychological barriers to success in women. In R. B. Kundsin (Ed.), *Women and success*. New York: Morrow, 1974.

Jones, A., & Seagull, A. A. Dimensions of the relationship between the black client and white therapist. *American Psychologist*, October 1977, *32* (10), 850–855.

King, M. C. The politics of sexual stereotypes. *The Black Scholar*, 1973, *4* (6–7), 12–23.

Lerman, H. Some thoughts on cross-gender psychotherapy. *Psychotherapy: Theory, Research and Practice*, Fall 1978, *15* (3), 248–250.

Sattler, J. M. The effects of therapist–client racial similarity. In A. S. Gurman & A. M. Razin (Eds.), *Effective psychotherapy*. New York: Pergamon Press, 1977, pp. 252–290.

Sherman, J., Koufacos, C. & Kenworthy, J. A. Therapists: Their attitudes and information about women. *Psychology of Women Quarterly*, Summer 1978, *2* (4), 299–313.

Turner, S., & Armstrong, S. Cross-racial psychotherapy: What the therapists say. *Psychotherapy: Theory, Research and Practice*, Fall 1981, *18* (3), 375–378.

Vanderson, J. Psychological determinants. In R. B. Kundsin, (Ed.), *Women and success*. New York: Morrow, 1974.

Vontress, C. E. Cultural barriers in the counseling relationship. *Personnel and Guidance Journal*, 1969, *48*, 11–17.

Wolken, G. H., Morwaki, S., & Williams, J. Race and social class as factors in the orientation toward psychotherapy. *Journal of Counseling Psychology*, 1973, *20* (4), 312–316.

■ four
GENDER ISSUES

■ 10

Hidden Assumptions in Theory and Research on Women[1]

RHODA KESLER UNGER

The area known as the psychology of women has been recognized as a legitimate aspect of psychology since 1973, when Division 35 (The Psychology of Women) became an official part of the organizational structure of the discipline. Psychology of women grew out of feminist disenchantment with traditional psychology. While there appears to be general agreement as to the problems of mainstream psychology, however, no such agreement appears to exist as to how the psychology of women should proceed. Kahn and Jean (1983) have attempted to analyze positions within the psychology of women in terms of a dichotomy—separatism versus integration with psychology as a whole. Theorists within the field seem to vary in terms of whether sex and gender can be studied within the traditional constructs of psychology; whether integration of content and method area is possible only after sex equality has been achieved within psychology and within society as a whole; or whether separation from mainstream psychology is

1. Parts of this paper were presented at the Symposium "The Future of the Psychology of Women: Separation, Integration, Elimination?", American Psychological Association, Annual Meeting, Washington, D.C., August 1982, and at the Meeting of the Association for Women in Psychology, Boston, Mass., March 1981.

necessary with the development of a field based on women's biology and experience. Each of these positions has different implications for theory and practice within the field as well as for interactions between those within it and mainstream psychology. This chapter is an attempt to explore and resolve some of these apparent dichotomies.

In order to know where we are going it is necessary to know where we have been as well as where we are now. Many attempts have been made in the past few years to define the psychology of women. A summary of my own such attempts include discussion of the "name controversy" (Unger, 1979a); citation analysis of texts in the field (which appears to indicate that we have been studying a "psychology of girls" rather than a psychology of women; Unger, 1982); and brief surveys of the field in terms of its historical and methodological development (Unger, in press).

All of these attempts have convinced me that the field cannot be wholly encompassed by any of these procedures. Nevertheless, we have reached a point in the profession in which two journals publish articles primarily in the psychology of women and program committees are able to put together large bodies of scholarly work on an annual basis. It appears, therefore, that some level of agreement exists about what constitutes scholarship in the field even if the definition is primarily denotative.

There seems to be general agreement that work on any aspect of sex discrimination (whether attitudinal, perceptual-cognitive, behavioral, or structural-systemic), on aspects of the life experiences of particular women or women in general (this work may be either intrapsychic or behavioral in focus and may be either theoretical or applied), and on sex differences (independent of the explanation for such differences or their value or policy implications) constitutes legitimate concerns for the psychology of women. It is more difficult to deal with recent works that critique research practices and the underlying ideology of research in psychology (cf. McHugh, Koeske, & Frieze, 1981; O'Leary, 1981; Sherif, 1979; Unger, in press; Wallston, 1981). In fact, as I will discuss later, the problem of whether or not to identify such critiques with the psychology of women alone is one of the questions that makes issues involving the appropriate direction of the field so difficult to resolve.

Recently, I have been attempting to understand the direction of the field by means of an analysis of the ideological assumptions that seem to underlie much of the recent work within it. This kind of analysis appears to have a number of potentially fruitful uses. It may help in understanding why some research questions are especially popular whereas others (seemingly as interesting) have been virtually ignored. I would argue that questions that have received a great deal of scholarly attention are those that mesh with one or more ideological assumptions implicit in a feminist orientation in psychology. Ideological bias appears to influence the kinds of research questions asked as well as the interpretation of the answers obtained (Unger, in press). There is no *a priori* reason to suppose that feminist researchers are any more immune from the effects of their values than are our peers who are committed to other covert ideologies.

Some of the ideological assumptions of a feminist orientation in psychology are probably relatively independent of each other, and others, carried to a logical conclusion, may be mutually contradictory. Analysis of these mixed values may be helpful in understanding the sources of some of the controversies within the psychology of women.

It should be clear, of course, that not everyone who contributes to the psychology of women would consider herself or himself a feminist and that values may be held independent of whether or not one identifies with the label. I also do not wish to make value judgments about the kind or number of implicit assumptions held. Instead, I wish to use this kind of analysis in the interest of greater understanding of the field in the hope that more knowledge about ourselves will lead to more informed choices about the directions we wish to take.

I propose that the value system by which feminist research may be characterized includes at least six relatively independent dimensions. Feminist psychologists may be distinguished from other psychologists (who may be interested in similar content areas, use similar methodologies, and conduct equally important work in the psychology of women) by a greater tendency to endorse statements of the following kind:

1. Conscious awareness is an important source of personal and social change.
2. Factors such as luck or the influence of powerful others are important for understanding individuals' efforts to control their environment and the outcome of such efforts.
3. Power must be viewed in terms of societal structure as well as the degree of control over circumstances the individual perceives herself or himself to possess.
4. Social/environmental causal mechanisms are more useful for understanding sex-related behaviors than are biological mechanisms.

5. Seeking social change is a legitimate aspiration both within and outside of the psychological establishment.
6. It is important to question the way our knowledge base is generated and maintained.

These position statements represent ideological values associated with a feminist orientation in psychology. As values they may be held implicitly without individual awareness of their influence on one's work. They may serve, however, as a place from which to examine the present sex-related reality which the psychology of women has helped to construct and with which it must deal. Contradictions within and between values and between some feminist values and those that are the product of traditional socialization within psychology help explain some of the apparent conceptual confusion within the field as well as giving it much of its intellectual energy. I shall now examine each of these positions in some detail.

THE IMPORTANCE OF CONSCIOUS AWARENESS

Belief in the powerful role of conscious awareness in behavior may be one of the most important but unexamined values in American society as a whole and in psychology in particular. For example, it is difficult to argue for the importance of a college education or for any particular course of study within the liberal arts curriculum unless one believes that an expanded base of knowledge will offer the individual a greater range of choices in his or her later life. Clinical psychology stresses the importance of early experience and intrapsychic dynamics as major influences on subsequent behavior, but also assumes that awareness of such forces will lead to beneficial behavioral change. The unexamined assumption here is that there is a strong positive connection between knowledge and the ability or willingness to use that knowledge.

It is obvious that the earliest feminist focus on consciousness raising assumed this position of "you shall know the truth and the truth shall make you free." More current related trends within the psychology of women include attention to the organization of the self system (Sherif, 1982) and the relationship between the way one organizes the self in terms of gender schemata and perceptions about other aspects of sex-related reality (Bem, 1981).

Unexamined assumptions about the importance of awareness in the reorganization of the self may lead to some conflicts with other feminist priorities. Possibly the most important unanswered question is: What is the relationship between self-knowledge and social change? It is distressing to note that researchers who have been largely responsible for the development of the concept of androgyny have repeatedly stated that there is no necessary relationship between judgments about the self in terms of sex-related traits and attitudes about the rights and roles of women in society (Helmreich, 1982; Spence & Helmreich, 1978), yet the area remains one of the most popular in the psychology of women with little apparent concern about this lack of relationship.

The focus on the self in terms of intrapsychic properties—a focus shared with psychology as a whole—can easily lead to person-blame approaches to problems. Kahn (1972) has charged that psychologists are more willing to blame individuals for their difficulties with society than are members of the general public. Many concepts derived from a person-centered focus on women, while not formulated as faults or character weaknesses, can be used to blame the victim. Concepts such as fear of success, lack of assertiveness, and currently androgyny (when femininity is viewed as a lack of socially desirable instrumental characteristics) are the most widely cited concepts derived from the psychology of women to be found in the mainstream psychological literature. Such concepts appear to be incorporated into psychology much faster than other aspects of feminist analysis, especially those concerned with the role played by societal structures.

Intrapsychic explanations for the differences in the lives of women and men may be more easily incorporated into psychology because they fit neatly into the implicit value framework of the discipline. Such intrapsychic formulations are also convenient in maintaining the status quo since they make it appear that the need for change resides within the individual. More powerful individuals within the system and the system itself are, therefore, safely exonerated from responsibility or blame.

One can argue that scholars are not responsible for the uses to which their ideas are put. Feminist scholars, however, have become aware of the dilemmas produced by too exclusive focus on internal dynamics. For example, whereas mainstream critics have concentrated on the methodological limitations of androgyny as an operationalized concept (Pedhazur & Tetenbaum, 1979), feminist analyses have concerned themselves with its relationship to other aspects of gender-related reality (Spence & Helmreich, 1978), with its relationship to situational context (Kaplan, 1979), and with the social judgments made about males and females who display gender-inappropriate traits (Massad, 1981).

THE CONNECTION BETWEEN
OUTPUT AND OUTCOME

Belief in the efficacy of self-awareness would appear to be connected closely with a belief in the power of conscious effort to change life circumstances. Feminist scholars, however, are particularly sensitive to the impact of forces which are not under the direct control of the individual. This sensitivity may be due to the fact that female researchers—although a relatively privileged group of women in our society—have had fewer experiences of success following their efforts than have their male peers (Astin, 1969, 1973; Helson, 1978). There appear to be fewer connections between professional output and professional rewards for women than for men. Carolyn Sherif (1982) aptly noted that we must also look at the nature of the rewards offered. Women are more likely to be offered prestige rather than actual positions of power.

A number of concepts related to the connection between output and outcome are important research areas in the psychology of women. Of special interest is the concept of learned helplessness when it is viewed in the context of social processes. Learned helplessness has important implications for understanding battered women (Walker, 1978), depression (Radloff, 1975), and achievement decrements in girls in the middle school years (Dweck, Goetz, & Strauss, 1980). In a feminist analysis, learned helplessness or the related variable, external attribution for success and internal attribution for failure, is viewed as a cognitive mediator of behavior induced by consistent societal patterns of reinforcement and non-reinforcement directed toward individuals comprising a particular social category.

Research on the perceived connection between effort and reward illustrates one of the major strengths of the feminist perspective in psychology. Researchers have sought outside of the person and outside of the laboratory for the sources of cognitions that appear to be more characteristic of one sex than the other. Thus, researchers have focused on the sex-specific behaviors of teachers (Serbin, Conner, & Iler, 1979) and on the willingness of husbands to use physical force (Frieze & McHugh[2]) in their analyses of girls and women's behaviors. This focus on the real-life situation of individuals is particularly important under conditions where personal effort is ineffective or maladaptive when the social system itself remains unchanged.

SOURCES OF POWER

Although power has received great attention since the beginning of the present era of feminist scholarship (Polk, 1974), analyses of power may produce some of the most potentially divisive problems for those in the field of the psychology of women. Feminist ideology stresses power as a societal and political concept. Psychological ideology, however, tends to view power in more personal terms. Sources of power are looked for within the person and perceptions of power are often confused with real power. Intrapsychic power is frequently termed *control*, but specification of terminology does not resolve the issues here.

The reliance of psychology on manipulated variables, control, and laboratory research has helped to obscure the role of prior relationships within the social system. Thus, most of the work analyzing sex-related differences in power within the family, within institutional structures such as the work world, and within society as a whole has come from sociology. Nevertheless, power and status can be dealt with within more purely psychological paradigms. It is particularly noteworthy that when status information about the sexes is manipulated, status rather than sex accounts for virtually all the differential perceptions about women and men found (Eagly & Wood, in press).

Although feminist scholars are probably less likely than other psychologists to confuse perceptions of power with real power, we may share with other psychologists a general tendency to believe that some perceptions of power are more normative than others. For example, most studies of locus of control accept the notion that an internal locus is healthier. Examination of the literature on locus of control over the past ten years reveals a large number of studies aimed at demonstrating or altering external perceptions

---

2. Frieze, I. H., & McHugh, M. C. Violence and other bases of power in marriage. Paper presented at the Meeting of the American Psychological Association, Los Angeles, August 1981.

of control in various "pathological" populations (Unger[3]). The populations studied include the institutionalized mentally ill, prisoners, the elderly, blacks and other minorities, and obese women. However, perceptions of control under conditions where it is actually lacking may be quite maladaptive. Thus, Felton and Kahana (1974) found that among the institutionalized aged, those who were the most external with respect to a number of daily problems also reported the most positive adjustment to their situation. Externalized system blame has also been found to be positively associated with social activism in blacks (Gurin, Gurin, Lao, & Beattie, 1969). Under some life circumstances external locus of control is merely indicative of good reality testing. The specification of unique life circumstances is a component of feminist scholarship, but it is one which conflicts with the prescription of our profession to uncover "universal" laws of behavior.

NATURE–NURTURE AND SEX-RELATED DIFFERENCES

It is probably not necessary to document the strong belief in environmental causality that underlies much research in the psychology of women. Arguments about nature–nurture are probably the most openly discussed controversies within the field. It has been difficult for feminists who stress the importance of some biological factors to defend their views from critics within the field concerned with the maintenance of sexist biases. Some resolution of the problem may be provided by making a distinction between attending to sex differences and statements about their causal mechanisms and societal value. On the one hand, one can note characteristic sex-related differences and argue for their evolutionary utility (Hoyenga & Hoyenga, 1979) or for their social value. At the opposite extreme, one can stress how few sex-related differences exist (the point made most impressively by Maccoby and Jacklin, 1974) and deny the social utility of any categorization based on biological sex alone. Several trends within psychology and women's studies, however, indicate that arguments about the existence of sex differences and interpretations about the meaning of

3. Unger, R. K. Controlling out the obvious: Power, status, and social psychology. Paper presented at the Meeting of the American Psychological Association, Washington, D.C., August 1982.

such differences are more independent of each other than we may have previously perceived.

A recent development I find particularly frightening may be found in the literature on stereotyping. A number of researchers have begun to characterize sex stereotypes as "normative" (Martin & Halverson, 1981; McCaulay, Stitt, & Segal, 1980). This terminology is apparently used to indicate that stereotypic responses are a product of accurate social awareness rather than individual pathology. Such stereotypes are said to have utility for the holder in terms of predictive accuracy because of the differential distribution of social roles on the basis of race and sex. The implication of this terminology, however, is to focus attention away from stereotyping as a psychological problem. If the individual who stereotypes is seen as "normal," less attention need be paid to societal systems which facilitate the generation and maintenance of such cognitive judgments.

How we view sex differences probably determines what questions we ask about them. Researchers who see stereotyping as normative omit the question of whether there is a veridical connection between what is perceived and what is. They are unlikely to examine the conditions under which stereotypical perceptions are disconfirmed. Such questions as what is the critical mass of disconfirming examples necessary to alter a stereotype, how much and what kind of information must be provided by the individual who fails to behave according to his or her categorical label, and what situational or personality factors lead to a search for additional, more veridical information have been neglected. These questions are, of course, critical ones for feminist scholarship.

Even self-proclaimed students of women's studies do not agree about the number of sex-related differences to be found, the causal mechanisms underlying such differences, and their importance to society. Catherine Stimpson[4] has recently noted the existence of two basic positions on sex differences within women's studies: the minimalist and the maximalist postion. Minimalists stress that nurture means more than nature; that sex differences are the results of culture, education, and socialization; and that biological differences, especially those associated with reproduction, have been inflated. My suggestion that gender (societally specific characteristics prescribed for each sex and associated with masculinity and femininity

4. Stimpson, C. The new scholarship about women. Paper presented at the Graduate Center, CUNY, New York, October 1981.

within all cultures) rather than sex (the biological and/or stimulus aspects of being a male or female) encompass the content area of the psychology of women reflected this position (Unger, 1979b).

The maximalist position, however, is also espoused by individuals who consider themselves feminist (cf. Rossi, 1977). This position stresses that cultural development reflects biological priorities and that social and political equality of the sexes does not necessarily rest on biological sameness. The feminist position in this area argues that scholars should uncover and praise the strengths of women on both a biological and a cultural level rather than downplaying women's differences from men. The maximalist position exemplifies an extreme form of scholarly separatism.

Neither the minimalist nor the maximalist position seems to be related logically to any particular theoretical or political position within the study of the psychology of women. In fact, some of the sex differences stressed by radical feminists are surprisingly similar to those espoused by unabashed sexists. The groups differ on the value of sex-related traits to individuals of the opposite sex and on the value of the various traits to society as a whole.

If one carries this kind of analysis somewhat further, we may find that there is also no necessary connection between belief in many versus few sex-related differences, between one's position on the biological or social causality of such differences, and attitudes about needed social change in the relationship between the sexes. We may have been misled about their degree of logical cohesiveness because feminist ideology appears to mandate consistency in these areas.

THE NEED FOR SOCIAL CHANGE

Possibly the one characteristic that most feminist scholars would agree upon is the need for social change. But even this area is more problematic than we may like to admit. The limits of such change is a relatively undiscussed issue. For example, if society became "sex-blind" and one's social identity as a male or female was no longer a basis for one's role in society, would the need for any more social change still exist? A logical consequence of a minimalist position on sex-related differences is that a great deal of further social change would not have to take place once society ceased to use sex as a basis for social categorization. Females and males would then be free to seek roles, occupations, and so on which were suited to their particular needs and talents.

The dilemma here is the kind of a society in which they would be finding their niche. What kinds of characteristics would be desirable in such a society? If, as recent research seems to suggest, instrumental traits are more socially acceptable in females than affective traits are in males (Jones, Chernovetz, & Hansson, 1978; Massad, 1981), then the logical termination of a sex-blind system is a "masculinized" society. If one assumes, moreover, that some kind of differentiation into categories is natural to society, as is suggested by Brewer's (1979) analysis of in-group bias in intergroup situations, then some categories of individuals will always be valued more than others. It is likely that individuals with stereotypic masculine characteristics, whatever their biological sex, will be the preferred group. This is not the kind of society in which I would like to live.

An additional issue in this area is whether social change should be limited to sex-related issues, or must one concern oneself with issues of race and social class as well? A partial resolution of this problem depends on whether one defines the psychology of women as a content area or as a study of processes. Social processes do not have a sex, a race, or a social class. Thus, the same kind of analysis (with revisions) may be applied to many social groups. Such a generalist focus—as contrasted to a particularist one—is unnecessary if one limits oneself to females as a subject area.

HOW SCIENCE WORKS

As I noted earlier, much dissatisfaction has been expressed recently with traditional experimental models for research in psychology. This model has been criticized for obscuring the social realities it purports to examine (Sherif, 1979) and for creating some of the phenomena it purports to uncover (Unger, 1981). Researchers in social cognition (cf. Hamilton, 1979) have demonstrated that congitive biases are much more pervasive than previously believed.

Some feminist scholars have stressed that science fails to advance because of institutionalized processes as well as methodological flaws (cf. Payer, 1977). Analysis of citations within mainstream psychology indicates that feminist analyses have had little impact on the rest of the field (Unger,

1982). Lack of legitimacy in terms of citations for the psychology of women mau be seen as unimportant as long as the relevant phenomena are explored, but earlier waves of feminist awareness in psychology failed to persist (Sherif, 1979; Shields, 1975). Crane (1972) has suggested that theoretical frameworks fail because they fail to acquire new individuals who retain that perspective. Hence, how science operates may be an important concern for feminist scholars, but it is one that has received little attention from them. Feminist researchers may not believe that science "works" as well as their mostly male peers do, but they do believe that it works. Clinging to this belief may have profound personal and professional consequences.

THE VALUE OF UNDERSTANDING IDEOLOGY

It is important to reiterate that ideology is implicit, not often attended to, and frequently inconsistent. Ideology may also be held independently of the nomenclature by which people choose to label themselves or others. The issues of how ideology changes and the conditions for such change are still unresolved. I have made no attempt to provide a litmus test for loyalty to feminist principles.

Analysis of belief structures, however, may provide us with some criteria as to what the psychology of women is and where it is going. It should be clear from this analysis that feminist psychology and the psychology of women are not totally overlapping categories. It should also be clear from this analysis that the value of work to the field cannot be determined by the degree to which it adheres to feminist principles.

Nevertheless, some areas of research in the field have developed more rapidly than others because they support some aspect of an implicit feminist value structure. For example, a great deal of attention has been paid to innumerable aspects of societal sexism. Sexism has been shown to exist from "womb to tomb" (Unger, 1979a). Presumably, such studies have been motivated by the desire to demonstrate how unequitable sex-biased beliefs and behaviors are. It is difficult to convince oneself that such evidence will not inevitably change people's view of the sexes. It also appears to be difficult to convince those doing research and practice in the psychology of women that there is no necessary connection between personal and social change nor between the presence or absence of gender-appropriate traits and ideology about what kind of social system is desirable.

There is no great evidence for a connection between what we know to be true and what scholarship says we know. Barbara Wallston (1981) has addressed this issue in terms of using personal experience as a method for generating questions. We need to come to grips with the issue of who decides what is legitimate knowledge and the criteria by which such determinations are made (Payer, 1977). While this issue is a critical one for all new areas of study, it is particularly problematic for feminist scholarship, which is ambivalent on the issue of personal success and elitism and mistrustful of any attempts to define standards of excellence.

Issues of elitism and legitimacy need to be dealt with openly because of the nature of scholarship as it is rather than as we would like it to be. The psychology of women as an organized part of psychology partakes of the nature of scholarship as it is. Decisions are made about what gets published and what gets cited. Absolute separation between spheres of scholarship cannot and should not be maintained. Information has a way of "leaking" from the psychology of women to the mainstream literature. As I have noted earlier, there is selectivity in terms of what aspects of the field are most easily integrated. This aspect of how science works is not under our control. Concepts that are most easily integrated into mainstream psychology are those that share paradigmatic similarity with concepts currently popular in the field, those that are most concordant with the implicit ideology of psychology, and those whose sources lend those who cite them stature and credibility.

Can we assume then that total integration is merely a matter of time? Although I would have said so once, I am no longer convinced that such integration is either possible or desirable without at least major changes in psychology as it presently exists. Psychology will have particular difficulty incorporating some of the things we take to be true based on feminist assumptions. For example, psychology will have trouble assimilating the view that personal perspective alters what can be known and that psychology can be neither objective nor value-free. Mainstream psychology will also have difficulty incorporating a political perspective—the view that to examine is to evaluate and that such evaluation always has politicosocial implications when humans are the object of scrutiny.

It may be argued that whereas the psychology of women is a legitimate part of psychology, feminist psychology has not yet secured such legitimacy. What will be the result if feminist research is not valued in its own right? Feminist researchers could find themselves adding to their own knowledge, but not to scholarship with its organizational and historical continuity. If some ideas are recognized, but feminism is not credited with them, any changes are likely to be selective in nature. On the other hand, if feminist research and researchers become too successful, we could lose the outsider's perspective that has enabled us to learn some of the lessons the rest of psychology needs to know. Integration into the field does not alter responsibility to other outsiders—women unable or unwilling to be part of organized psychology, less privileged women, and less privileged people in general.

The issue of integration, separation, or elimination is not one of choice alone. We are, however, responsible for analyzing the implications of ideological, scholarly, and political commitments. Those who identify with the psychology of women comprise the largest body of socially aware critics within organized psychology. Criticism of ourselves as well as of others will not destroy us. Refusal to do so may.

REFERENCES

Astin, H. S. *The woman doctorate in America*. New York: Russell Sage Foundation, 1969.

Astin, H. S. Career profiles of woman doctorates. In A. Rossi & A. Calderwood (Eds.), *Academic women on the move*. New York: Russell Sage Foundation, 1973.

Bem, S. L. Gender schema theory: A cognitive account of sex typing. *Psychological Review*, 1981, *88*, 354–364.

Brewer, M. B. In-group bias in the minimal intergroup situation: A cognitive motivational analysis. *Psychological Bulletin*, 1979, *86*, 307–324.

Crane, D. *Invisible colleges: Diffusion of knowledge in scientific communities*. Chicago: University of Chicago Press, 1972.

Dweck, C. S., Goetz, T. E., & Strauss, N. L. Sex differences in learned helplessness: IV. An experimental and naturalistic study of failure generalization and its mediators. *Journal of Personality and Social Psychology*, 1980, *38*, 441–452.

Eagly, A. H., & Wood, W. Gender and influenceability: Stereotype vs. behavior. In V. E. O'Leary, R. K. Unger, & B. S. Wallston (Eds.), *Women, gender, and social psychology*. Hillsdale, N.J.: Lawrence Erlbaum Associates, in press.

Felton, B., & Kahana, E. Adjustment and situationally-bound locus of control among institutionalized aged. *Journal of Gerontology*, 1974, *29*, 295–301.

Gurin, R., Gurin, G., Lao, R. C., & Beattie, M. Internal-external control in the motivational dynamics of Negro youth. *Journal of Social Issues*, 1969, *25*, 29–53.

Hamilton, D. L. A cognitive-attributional analysis of stereotyping. In L. Berkowitz (Ed.), *Advances in experimental social psychology* (Vol. 12). New York: Academic Press, 1979.

Helmreich, R. L. On the distinction between sex-role attitudes and sex-linked traits and their stability. In P. W. Berman & E. R. Ramey (Eds.), *Women: A developmental perspective*. Washington, D.C.: NIH Publication No. 82–2298, 1982.

Helson, R. M. Creativity in women. In J. Sherman & F. Denmark (Eds.), *The psychology of women: Future directions of research*. New York: Psychological Dimensions, 1978.

Hoyenga, K. B., & Hoyenga, K. T. *The question of sex differences: Psychological, cultural, and biological issues*. Boston: Little, Brown, 1979.

Jones, W. H., Chernovetz, M. E. O'C., & Hansson, R. O. The enigma of androgyny: Differential implications for males and females? *Journal of Consulting and Clinical Psychology*, 1978, *46*, 298–313.

Kahn, A. S., & Jean, P. J. Integration and elimination or separation and redefinition: The future of the psychology of women as a discipline. *Signs*, 1983, *8*.

Kahn, R. L. The justification of violence: Social problems and social resolutions. *Journal of Social Issues*, 1972, *28*, 155–175.

Kaplan, A. G. (Ed.). Psychological androgyny: Further implications. *Psychology of Women Quarterly*, 1979, *3* (3).

Maccoby, E. E., & Jacklin, C. N. *The psychology of sex differences*. Stanford: Stanford University Press, 1974.

Martin, C. L., & Halverson, C. F. Jr. A schematic processing model of sex typing and stereotyping in children. *Child Development*, 1981, *52*, 1119–1134.

Massad, C. M. Sex role identity and adjustment during adolescence. *Child Development*, 1981, *52*, 1290–1298.

McCaulay, C., Stitt, C. L., & Segal, M. Stereotyping: From prejudice to prediction. *Psychological Bulletin*, 1980, *87*, 195–208.

McHugh, M. C., Koeske, R. D., & Frieze, I. H. Guidelines for nonsexist research. Report of the Task Force of Division 35 of APA, December, 1981.

O'Leary, V. E. (Ed.). Special section on feminist research. *Psychology of Women Quarterly*, 1981, *5*, 595–653.

Payer, M. E. Is traditional scholarship value free? Towards a critical theory. *Papers from the Scholar and the Feminist. IV: Connecting theory, practice, and values*. New York: The Women's Center, Barnard College, 1977.

Pedhazur, E. J., & Tetenbaum, T. J. Bem Sex Role Inventory: A theoretical and methodological critique. *Journal of Personality and Social Psychology*, 1979, *37*, 996–1016.

Polk, B. B. Male power and the women's movement. *Journal of Applied Behavioral Science*, 1974, *10*, 415–431.

Radloff, L. Sex differences in depression: The effects of occupation and marital status. *Sex Roles*, 1975, *1*, 249–265.

Rossi, A. S. A biosocial perspective on parenting. *Daedalus*, 1977, *106*, 1–31.

Serbin, L., Conner, J. M., & Iler, I. Sex-stereotyped and non-stereotyped introduction of new toys in the preschool classroom: An observational analysis of teacher behavior and its effects. *Psychology of Women Quarterly*, 1979, *4*, 261–265.

Sherif, C. W. Bias in psychology. In J. Sherman & E. T. Beck (Eds.), *The prism of sex: Essays in the sociology of knowledge*. Madison: University of Wisconsin Press, 1979.

Sherif, C. W. Needed concepts in the study of gender identity. *Psychology of Women Quarterly*, 1982, *6*, 375–398.

Shields, S. A. Functionalism, Darwinism, and the psychology of women: A study in social myth. *American Psychologist*, 1975, *30*, 739–754.

Spence, J. T., & Helmreich, R. L. *Masculinity and femininity: Their psychological dimensions, correlates, and antecedents*. Austin: University of Texas Press, 1978.

Unger, R. K. *Female and male: Psychological perspectives*. New York: Harper & Row, 1979. (a)

Unger, R. K. Toward a redefinition of sex and gender. *American Psychologist*, 1979, *34*, 1084–1094. (b)

Unger, R. K. Sex as a social reality: Field and laboratory research. *Psychology of Women Quarterly*, 1981, *5*, 645–653.

Unger, R. K. Advocacy versus scholarship revisited: Issues in the psychology of women. *Psychology of Women Quarterly*, 1982, *7*, 5–17.

Unger, R. K. Through the looking glass: No Wonderland yet! Presidential Address to Division 35 of APA. *Psychology of Women Quarterly*, in press.

Walker, L. *The battered woman*. New York: Harper & Row, 1978.

Wallston, B. S. What are the questions in psychology of women? A feminist approach to research. *Psychology of Women Quarterly*, 1981, *5*, 597–617.

■11

Working Women and Stress

LAURA J. SOLOMON

Stress is perhaps the most pervasive health-related problem experienced by contemporary society. Aside from the discomfort associated with acute and chronic stress, it has been identified as a risk factor in numerous physical and psychological disorders (e.g., headaches, insomnia, ulcers, coronary heart disease, anxiety disorders). Even some short-term attempts to cope with stress have led to health problems (e.g., drug abuse, alcohol abuse, excessive smoking).

In general, the mental health profession has viewed stress-related health problems as the consequence of the hard-working, post-industrial masculine life style. Psychophysiological disorders tend to be more prevalent among males, particularly among those engaged in "stressful" occupations (e.g., air traffic controllers, combat soldiers). The ambitious, overworked, male business executive is often lauded as the image of success. In contrast, the image of the stressed female seems to highlight the fears and anxieties associated with an inability to handle the most mundane tasks. Interestingly, a closer look at the small but expanding literature on working women and stress reveals a different but still disturbing picture.

I will address four issues in this chapter. First, I will very briefly review past findings on women and stress and consider how the female sex role might help explain the relationship. Second, I will discuss the changes in the number of women in the salaried work force and suggest what stressors might result from these changes. Third, I will consider how the traditional sex roles might serve to enhance the stress of the working woman. Finally, I will suggest some ways to possibly reduce or prevent stress in working women.

PAST FINDINGS

Traditionally, women have reported to mental health centers with stress-related complaints at a higher frequency than have men (Gove & Gurken, 1977; Webb & Allen, 1979). While there are several ways to account for this sex difference, the stressors associated with the female sex role, no doubt, play some part. The female sex role encourages women to take primary responsibility for the rearing of children and the keeping of the household. If one examines the characteristics of the role, one can find numerous occupational stressors inherent in the homemaker-mother position. Among the stressors which are frequently evident in the homemaker role are the following: underutilization of educational skills, excessive hours of work, lack of recognition for accomplishments, lack of monetary rewards, reponsibility for the welfare of other people (most notably, the children). According to French[1] these are many of the factors that have been identified as contributing to stress in the work environment. Additionally, Ferre (1976) reported that many housewives experience stress because they find housework monotonous and unrewarding and because of the social isolation often associated with the traditional homemaker role. The fact that the homemaker-caretaker duties typically fall into the hands of the woman rather than the man may explain why Gove (1973) found that the married state produces greater stress-related morbidity (suicide attempts, illnesses related to alcohol and tobacco, illnesses requiring prolonged care) among women and among men.

    While women have continued to maintain the role of primary homemaker, the number of women in the salaried work force has increased dramatically in the past 30 years. By 1970, 50 percent of American women ages 18 to 64 were in the paid work force, compared to 30 percent in 1940.

1. French, J. R. P. Job demands and worker health: Introduction. Presented at Annual Meeting of American Psychological Association, Washington, D.C., 1976.

The majority of women employed in 1970 worked in the areas of clerical work, sales, teaching, and health care (U.S. Bureau of the Census, 1973). These particular occupations tend to fall within the lower range of the pay scale. The 1980 census shows an even more marked increase in women in the salaried work force.

THE EFFECTS OF MORE WOMEN WORKING

The effect of this increase in the number of women in the work force has been that large numbers of women actually have two full-time jobs. Women did not shed the role of homemaker-mother, but rather they added the role associated with a job or career. The International Labor Office has calculated that women throughout the world work approximately 80 hours per week while men work approximately 50 hours per week. One might conclude on the basis of this information alone that the dual-job woman has considerable demands on her time.

The rapid influx of women to the paid work force encouraged many researchers to make comparisons between the stress experienced by employed women and the stress experienced by housewives. As one might expect from such global comparisons, the results are mixed. In general, and this is a rather sweeping generalization, housewives tend to fare more poorly than employed women on numerous physical and psychological measures. For example, Chambers (1972) and Parry, Balter, and Mellinger (1973) found housewives to be slightly more likely than employed women to use minor tranquilizers, sedatives, sleeping pills, and antidepressants. Welch and Booth (1977), using several measures of emotional stress and physical illness, found that women employed full-time for more than one year were healthier than either women employed for less than one year or housewives. Unemployed housewives (i.e., women who worked in the past but did not currently work outside the home) had the highest proportion of stress-related disorders. Cumming, Lazer, and Chisholm (1975) revealed that suicide rates in general were higher for housewives than for employed women, and most studies (e.g., Brown, Bhrolchain, & Harris, 1975; Gove & Gurken, 1977; Lowenthal & Berkman, 1967) found that employed women showed fewer signs of psychiatric impairment than did housewives.

This picture, however, is not complete and we cannot conclude that employed women are less stressed than housewives. First of all, it is important to note that these studies were cross-sectional rather than longitudinal, so one cannot be sure of causation. That is, it could be the case that healthier women tend to join the paid work force while less healthy women remain at home. Second, some of the studies looked at visits to the doctor (either psychologist or physician) as a dependent measure, and it is likely that more housewives than working women can afford the time out to visit the doctor. Finally, a closer inspection of the literature reveals that the above results (that employed women appear healthier than housewives) tend to hold for women of higher socioeconomic status (SES), but not for lower SES women. In fact, in Waldron's[2] review of this literature, it was noted that marital satisfaction was higher for housewives in samples of lower-class women, while marital satisfaction was greater for employed women in a sample of higher SES women. Additionally, clerical workers (who fall at the low end of the pay scale) have a high suicide rate relative to most other occupations for women (female physicians and psychologists excluded). It is quite possible that women working in blue-collar and lower white-collar jobs are exposed to more physical and chemical occupational hazards, experience greater stress in response to more serious financial pressures, and, perhaps, experience role conflict as a source of stress. That is, it is likely that working women at the lower pay grades might in fact prefer the luxury of the sex-role stereotype that is modeled for them in contemporary television shows and commercials. The stressors, then, for lower SES women who work purely in response to economic pressure might include performing monotonous work at low paying jobs, while still being responsible for the household, and possibily all the while striving for the stereotypic feminine sex role that would simplify her life by allowing her to be dependent, passive, and weak.

And yet it is not just the lower SES woman who experiences stress at work. Welch and Booth (1977) found that there are no differences in frequency of psychiatric impairment between employed women and housewives (across SES level) when either the employed woman began work during the past year or when the employed woman was the mother of young children. In fact, Haynes and Feinleib (1980) reported that women who had three or more children and who had been working outside the home for more than half their adult life had a significantly

2. Waldron, I. Employment and health of women: An analysis of causal relationships. Paper presented at Annual Meeting of American Psychological Association, Toronto, Canada, 1978.

higher incidence of coronary heart disease than did childless working women or housewives with three or more children. Again, however, the women with children and low paying jobs (e.g., clerical and sales occupations) had the highest incidence of coronary heart disease. Conversely, women who worked part-time had the best psychological health (Ferre, 1976; Rapoport & Rapoport, 1978; Welch & Booth, 1977).

TRADITIONAL SEX ROLES
AND ENHANCED STRESS

These data, taken together, suggest that there is clearly something about the combination of the traditional homemaker role and the demands of employment that is associated with greater stress in lower SES women and the majority of women just beginning work or having the responsibilities of young children.

Many of these studies were done in the early and mid 1970s, and since that time more and more women have begun to enter the salaried work force at managerial, administrative, and executive levels. These nontraditional positions can be expected to generate new stressors for women. For example, the lack of appropriate female role-models from whom one can learn the ropes may make the struggle for advancement more ambiguous for women compared to their male counterparts. Exclusion from the informal male social networks may enhance her isolation and reduce the likelihood of successful coping through social support, a helpful stress-reduction technique. The expectation that colleagues may have about the feminine sex-role stereotype and the behavior of a person in an administrative position may create a double bind for a woman in that situation. Thus, the female executive may have to cope with others' beliefs that she is not cut out for the job. Finally, many executive women continue to experience the burden of the dual career with the associated time demands and responsibilities. And if the professional woman chooses to pursue her career goals without simultaneously pursuing more domestic interests (e.g., husband and children), she risks facing the pressures imposed by a family-oriented society which might lead her to believe that she will later regret her decision or, worse still, that there must be something wrong with her.

Given the likelihood of these serious stressors, most notably role conflict, time demands, and heightened responsibilities, what might the executive woman do? It is likely that she will model her behavior after the behavior of managerial or administrative level men. The result of that approach is already becoming evident as more women are beginning to display the coronary prone behavior pattern or Type A behavior. According to Rosenman, Brand, Jenkins, Friedman, Straus and Wurm, the Type A individual is work-oriented, ambitious, aggressive, competitive, hurried, impatient, and preoccupied with deadlines. Men displaying the Type A behavior pattern are twice as likely as other men to develop coronary heart disease. (This relationship holds after controlling for other risk factors such as smoking, obesity, and hypertension.) A study by Waldron, Zyzanski, Shekelle, Jenkins, Tannenbaum (1977) revealed that while employed adult women were slightly less Type A than were men, employed women were more Type A than were housewives. Additionally, Waldron (1976) reported that the ratio of male to female deaths is declining due to an increase in female death rates. She noted that "the rising female death rates reflect a trend for more and more women to include in their lifestyle various life-endangering habits which formerly have been more common among men." Here she includes the long-term rise in cigarette smoking and the increased tendency to observe Type A behavior in employed women. Waldron additionally noted that the "relative rise of arteriosclerotic heart disease in women may be due to the increased time pressures and role conflicts that have resulted as an increasing proportion of women have taken jobs while still carrying primary responsibility for housework and care of children."

If modeling male behavior does not appear promising in terms of reducing stress for the administrative woman, then what alternatives are left?

ALTERNATIVES FOR REDUCING STRESS

One possibility involves training women in various coping skills to reduce daily stress. Some coping skills addressed in the stress-management literature include relaxation training, cognitive restructuring, social support, time management, assertion training, and improving physical health habits. These types of interventions would require endless hours of teaching individuals (either singly or in groups) to better deal with stress. They are not very cost-effective given the widespread nature of the stress-related problems experienced by women. Additionally, the individual coping skills approach places responsibility for change completely on the shoulders of the women who are the victims. If societal roles for women contribute to stress-related problems on a large scale, then institutions greater than individual women have a role to play in reducing the stress women experience.

Organizational-level interventions may alleviate some of the stressors women face. On an organizational level one could consider altering the contingencies so that coronary prone behavior patterns would be reduced and positive health habits might be increased. Some corporations (e.g., Exxon, Metropolitan Life, Ford Motor Company, Johnson and Johnson) have taken steps to reduce health care costs and the costs of absenteeism by providing the financial resources to develop and implement health-promotion programs for their employees. A company commitment to healthy life styles, modeling of positive health behaviors by corporate executives, and strong incentives for health behavior change could potentially encourage working women to incorporate health-conducive habits into their daily activities.

Organizational interventions could also take the form of women's networks, established to enable women to provide social support for other women and to encourage joint problem-solving among women. Working women as a group could provide input regarding ways in which corporate management could reduce common stress problems. By actively proposing solutions to shared stressors, women could have a voice in altering their work environment and influencing corporate policy.

Organizational-level solutions to some of the time pressure problems experienced by working women include variable work schedules and day-care facilities at the work setting. Variable work schedules such as flextime, modified work weeks, and job sharing could enable women with children to juggle their multiple responsibilities with greater ease. You will recall that women working part-time outside the home displayed the best psychological health in several studies. Flexplace alternatives could allow women and men to work in their own homes, connected to the work setting by electronic media. This option might permit parents of young children to simultaneously meet child-care and occupational duties. Corporate day-care facilities could ensure that both male and female parents of young children could coordinate their schedules more effectively and thereby reduce some of the time pressures and worries associated with the responsibility for their children. Such organizational initiatives are only a few of the options that innovative companies could pursue in their efforts to reduce the stress experienced by working women.

On the broadest scale, the societal level, changes in traditional sex roles and responsibilities could decrease the stressors for working women. This might be best accomplished through direct modeling of nontraditional alternatives and through media depiction of realistic solutions to the dual-career dilemma.

Second, we might strive toward establishing monetary reinforcers for individuals who are working within the family unit. In that way, men or women choosing to work solely in the home could be compensated for working, thereby reducing the need for such persons to grudgingly enter the out-of-the-home work force.

Finally, we could encourage the acceptance of nontraditional "family" units (e.g., childless marriages, communal life styles, etc.), for these are logical alternatives that could reduce stress by decreasing the time demands and excessive responsibilities associated with the dual-career women. These solutions necessitate considerable social changes, but the current trends in stress-related morbidity and mortality in working women warrant large-scale adjustments.

REFERENCES

Brown, G. W., Bhrolchain, M. M., & Harris, T. Social class and psychiatric disturbance among women in an urban population. *Sociology*, 1975, 9, 225–254.

Chambers, C. D. An assessment of drug use in the general population. In J. Susman, (Ed.), *Drug use and social policy*. New York: AMS Press, 1972.

Cumming, E., Lazer, C., & Chisholm, L. Suicide as an index of role strain among employed and not employed married women in British Columbia. *Canadian Review of Sociology and Anthropology*, 1975, 12, 462–470.

Ferre, M. M. Working class jobs: Housework and paid work as sources of satisfaction. *Social Problems*, 1976, 23, 431–441.

Gove, W. R. Sex, marital status and mortality. *American Journal of Sociology*, 1973, 79, 45–67.

Gove, W. R., & Gurken, M. R. The effect of children and employment on the mental health of married men and women. *Social Forces*, 1977, 56, 66–76.

Haynes, S. G., & Feinleib, M. Women, work and coronary heart disease: Prospective findings from the Framingham heart study. *American Journal of Public Health*, 1980, *70*, 133–140.

Lowenthal, M. F., & Berkman, P. L. *Aging and mental disorder in San Francisco*. San Francisco: Jossey-Bass, 1967.

Parry, H. J., Balter, M. B., & Mellinger, G. D. National patterns of psychotherapeutic drug use. *Archives of General Psychiatry*, 1973, *28*, 769–783.

Rapoport, R. N., & Rapoport, R. Dual-career families: Progress and prospects. *Marriage and Family Review*, 1978, *1*, 1–12.

Rosenman, R. H., Brand, R. J., Jenkins, C. D., Friedman, M., Straus, R., & Wurm, M. Coronary heart disease in the Western Collaborative Group Study: Final follow-up experience of 8½ years. *Journal of the American Medical Association*, 1975, *233*, 872–877.

U.S. Bureau of the Census. *Census of the population: 1970, Subject reports, Final report PC (2)-7A, Occupational characteristics*. Washington, D.C.: U.S. Government Printing Office, 1973.

Waldron, I. Why do women live longer than men? *Social Science and Medicine*, 1976, *10*, 349–362.

Waldron, I., Zyzsanski, S., Shekelle, R. B., Jenkins, C. D., & Tannenbaum, S. The coronary-prone behavior pattern in employed men and women. *Journal of Human Stress*, 1977, *3*, 2–18.

Webb, L., & Allen, R. Sex differences in mental health. *Journal of Psychology*, 1979, *101*, 89–96.

Welch, S., & Booth, A. Employment and health among married women with children. *Sex Roles*, 1977, *3*, 385–397.

■ 12

A Feminist Approach to Math-anxiety Reduction

IRENE DEITCH

This last decade has generated considerable attention to the study of the relation of women and mathematics (Aldrich, 1982; Fennema[1]; Fox, 1980; Sherman, 1976, Stage, 1982). One consequence of this has been the investigation of the issue of "mathematics anxiety." Mathematics anxiety has alternatively been labeled as "number anxiety" (Aiken, 1976), a syndrome of emotional reactions to arithmetic and mathematics, and as "mathophobia," an impeditive dread of mathematics (Lazarus, 1975). Math anxiety has been described as "feelings of tension and anxiety that interfere with manipulation of numbers and the solving of mathematical problems in ordinary life and academic situations" (Richardson & Suinn, 1972). Tobias (1978) characterized math anxiety as an irrational fear of failure. She refers to this intense feeling as a "sudden death experience" (p. 45).

1. Fennema, E. Women and mathematics: New directions for future research. Paper presented at American Educational Research Association, New York, 1982.

MATH ANXIETY AS A FEMINIST ISSUE

Psychologists, educators, and feminists have been challenged by the disproportionate prevalence of math anxiety (and its counterpart, math avoidance) among women (Afflack, 1978; Kreinberg, 1976; Kvarnes, 1980; Liff, 1978). Caution must be exercised, however, against premature inferences that math anxiety is a "women's problem." Math anxiety has been noted among white and minority high school and undergraduate males (Auslander[2]; Betz, 1978). It was also determined that at one institution, college freshmen reported only low levels of math anxiety and that there were no sex differences (Resnick, Viehe, & Segal, 1982). While there is evidence that math anxiety interferes with enrollment and performance in math, there is some uncertainty as to the degree.

Suggestions that sex differences in math abilities are innate (Benbow & Stanley, 1980) tend to "blame the victim" and perpetuate myths in this area (Fennema & Sherman, 1977; Fox, Brody, & Tobin, 1980). Fox (1980) studied sex differences in mathematics and distinguished between studying math, learning math, and the aptitude for math. She found that differences that may exist can be explained by social conditioning. Test-taking strategies (Marshall[3]) may also influence performance. Evidence supporting a biological or genetic basis for sex differences is inconclusive.

Crucial to the study of math anxiety in women is an examination of those etiological and intervening factors contributing to and reinforcing this disorder. The cause and consequences of "math anxiety" must be determined so that appropriate intervention programs to reverse this pattern can be developed (Blum[4]; Brush, 1980; Lazarus, 1980; Stage[5]). Investigations in the area of math anxiety and math avoidance have examined its relationship to female mental health (Tobias, Donady, & Kogelman, 1979); fear of failure (Patty & Stafford, 1978); fear of success (Boswell, 1980; Caballero, Giles, & Shaver, 1975; Helson, 1971); sex-role typing (Bem & Lenney, 1976); parental expectations (Kaminski, Erikson, Ross, &

2. Auslander, S. B. Attitude change of some undergraduate students after intervention of a math clinic. Personal communication, October 20, 1979.
3. Marshall, S. Why do boys and girls select different distractors and problems? Report funded by the National Institute of Education, under Grant No. NIE-G-80-0095, and presented to the American Education Research Association, New York, 1982.

Bradfield, 1976); counselor bias (Casserly, 1975; Schlossberg & Pietrofesa, 1974); lack of teacher reinforcement (McLure & Piel, 1978); stereotyping of math and related subjects (Ernest, 1978; Fennema & Sherman, 1977); sexism in math textbooks and math tests (Federbush, 1974; Nibbelink & Mangru, 1978); differential experiences (Fennema & Sherman, 1978, Fennema, 1982; Parsons *et al,* 1976); limited participation in high school math courses (Eccles, 1982; Sells, 1980); lack of peer support (Boswell, 1980; Fox et al., 1980); and insufficient same-sex role models (Brush, 1980; Ernest, 1978). In a survey of earned doctorates, the trend as derived from the data, indicated that the proportion of doctorates granted to women increased from 1971 to 1981 in all major fields with the exception of the physical sciences and mathematics where the number of women remained constant. However, "the number of women doctorates in education more than doubled, while the corresponding number of men decreased" (National Research Council, 1981).

Clearly, socialization variables contribute to attitudes, feelings, cognitive styles, achievement, and involvement with mathematics. It may be presumed that the stronger the traditional same-sex typing (Bem & Lenney, 1976), the greater the susceptibility to the influence of "mathematics anxiety." Women's confidence and attraction to quantitative areas are undermined by the myths and stereotypes that math is a male domain (i.e., women don't have a head for numbers; it's not feminine to do well in math, etc.). Avoidance of math and related subjects by women leads to a systematic pattern of women's exclusion from economically feasible careers and promotional opportunities. Ultimately what is created are serious limitations on women's input in policy making and political power. Thus, the status quo is preserved.

The recommendations of the Carnegie Commission (1973) and the passage of the Women's Educational Equity Act in 1974 pointed up long-standing discriminatory educational policies and practices. To rectify the significant underrepresentation of women in higher education in the areas of math, science, and technologies, active recruitment and organizational support began. Additionally, Title IX sought to establish equal opportunity for women in academe by federally funded affirmative-action programs.

4. Blum, L. Educating college women in mathematics. (A report of an action program in progress. Proceedings of the conference, "Educating women for science: A continuous spectrum.") Mills College, April 20, 1976, unpublished.
5. Stage, E. Women and mathematics: Strategies for future program development based on research and successful program models. Paper presented at American Education Research Association, New York, March 1982.

Women in the over-35-year age category have been cited as the fastest growing segment of post-secondary students (Mezirow & Marsick, 1978; National Center for Education Statistics, 1979). However, underlying sexist attitudes—subtle and not so subtle—on the part of some college professors, administrators, and counselors toward women majoring in nontraditional academic areas, older women, and minority women creates a chilly climate for them (Project on the Status and Education of Women, 1982). Furthermore, course enrollment for women in elective areas of math is proportionately significantly lower. No matter how highly motivated and successful the academic performance, adult college women encounter different treatment when compared to male students and female students of a younger age.

CONFRONTING THE PROBLEM: MATH ANXIETY WORKSHOPS

A series of math-anxiety workshops was designed to attack maladaptive patterns of behavior consisting of learned misconceptions, inappropriate responses, and self-defeating attitudes. This intervention program led to the formation of a "women's group" which in every respect was an all women's project. This was essential. To achieve change required unlearning and relearning ego-enhancing behavior in a nonsexist context of support and reassurance. Predictably, what emerges is a consciousness-raising group given training in a repertoire of behavioral and cognitive skills so that the women could deal effectively with problems relating to math.

In an effort to encourage readers who might be interested in starting and running a similar program, a description of the project will be presented. These workshops are easily adaptable to other institutional settings with other target populations and for those with other types of academic anxiety.

The Participants and the Format

All adult women students who had entered or reentered college after a minimum of ten years of elapsed time were eligible for participation. Another criteria determining eligibility was that these adult students described themselves as fearful of math to the extent that they had developed elaborate strategies to avoid having to take it. For some, it meant even delaying enrollment in college.

Participants for the project were solicited by means of classroom announcements, advertisements in the campus newspaper, and recommendation by counselors and math instructors. A public college was selected since lower tuition costs encouraged the enrollment of adult women. This institution housed a day-care center on campus and provided for off-campus classroom facilities for those who might otherwise not consider this site geographically accessible. There was thus greater potential for recruiting the parent-as-student population.

Forty-five women between the ages of 32 and 48 were selected after screening interviews. Participants were informed that group discussion and behavioral training would be the focus of the sessions. There was to be no expectation that mathematical skills or tutoring would be included in the workshops.

Days and times of workshops were determined by the constraints placed on students by their families and academic demands. Students selected the group that best fit their priorities. Statistical analysis of demographic data collected for all group members revealed no significant variability between groups.

Screening interviews were conducted by adult college women who, like the potential members, were returnees to school, but were *not* math-anxious. Educational histories, psychological questionnaires, and informal and standardized tests were administered (Bem, 1974; Brush[6]; Richardson & Suinn, 1972; Suinn, 1972). Appropriate arrangements were made for those applicants who failed to meet the criteria for admission to the workshop.

Candidates indicated in their interviews whether they were pursuing the same academic goals that they had set in high school. The post-high school decade in no way represented a time for change or reconsideration of options based on the reality of job market trends or salaries; however, it seemed to provide an incubation period for strong feelings and attitudes toward mathematics and a generalization to math-related areas.

Workshop leaders received eight hours of training until an established level of proficiency was reached. Group dynamics skills were included in training sessions. Literature lists on women's groups and behavioral groups

6. Brush, L. Mathematics anxiety in college students. Additional data on Mars. Communication, 1976.

were recommended (Wolfe & Fodor, 1975; Wolpe & Lazarus, 1973) and participants were given instruction in the theory and application of behavioral (Horne[7]; Wolpe & Lazarus, 1973) and cognitive techniques (Meichenbaum[8]; Walen, DiGiuseppi, & Wessler, 1980). Guidelines were developed for each workshop session.

For "observers" and "recorders," training was given to a select group of women who would be asked to observe manifestations of behavioral tension. They had to meet the same criteria as workshop leaders to be eligible to participate.

Each workshop consisted of six to eight women. Assigned to each group was a workshop leader, a co-leader, an observer, and a recorder. The group was scheduled for a two-hour session each week for a period of six weeks. At the conclusion of each session members were given printed handouts for home use so that workshop learning was reinforced. Participants were encouraged to keep a journal focusing on their experiences and feelings.

Groups were trained in cognitive behavioral approaches to the reduction of math anxiety. Group discussions centered on material from their journals, issues that they faced as women in the various roles they played, unresolved conflicts that affected their academic progress, and career selections. Models for this aspect of the group were secured from Meichenbaum,[9] Tobias (1978), Tobias et al. (1979), and Walen et al. (1980).

In the course of the workshop series, three women had to withdraw. Medical problems, divorce, and full-time employment were the reasons cited. Two workshop members had applied for a leave of absence—the other had withdrawn from school. All had maintained contact with their group (a mimeographed roster of workshop members and phone numbers was circulated at the beginning of the program.)

One of the most realistic problems that arises in ongoing workshops is that of scheduling and time conflicts that may arise. For those women with families, their children's illness and academic pressure, health and social demands would often generate tension and occasion their absence. Holiday breaks caused interference with workshops, as well.

7. Horne, A. Counselor's manual for test anxiety study. Unpublished, Indiana State University, 1977.
8. Meichenbaum, D. Therapist manual for cognitive behavior modification. Unpublished materials, 1972.
9. Meichenbaum, *op. cit.*

COGNITIVE BEHAVIORAL TRAINING

Systematic Desensitization Techniques

Session 1   Only after rapport is established, leaders describe anxiety as a result of a learning process and desensitization as another learning process. The techniques are discussed briefly. A standardized mathematics anxiety hierarchy is distributed. The process of ordering the items and the necessity of adding or deleting items is explained. Relaxation training is given.

Session 2   Hierarchies are reviewed. Leaders check to see that all students have practiced relaxation techniques. Relaxation training with the hierarchy begins. As each student looks at her first item (least anxiety provoking), she is instructed to close her eyes and imagine it. Suggestions made to facilitate the process are "Imagine you are there . . . now . . . relax . . . feel yourself in the situation." If the student becomes mildly anxious she is asked to signal the leader by raising her right index finger. Students go through three items during this second session, closing with a successful experience, and a few minutes of positive reinforcement. They practice instructions until the next meeting.

Sessions 3–6   About five new items are worked out successfully for each session. Participants discuss the applicability of this technique for other situations in which they feel arousal of anxiety level. Personal situations in which there has been successful adaptation of this technique are shared.

Cognitive Restructuring Techniques

This approach is based on an extension of the principles of rational-emotive therapy (RET) (Ellis & Grieger, 1977; Wolfe & Fodor, 1975) and includes self-instructional training (Rogers & Craighead, 1977). Leaders use student experiences, self-statements, and thought processes to demonstrate adaptive and maladaptive behavior. Cognitive approaches attack the stereotypical beliefs held by members of the group. Monitoring of self-statements and self-instructional training encourages the application of this coping mechanism to other situations in which anxiety is generated.

The leader describes the rationale underlying the notion of anxiety in general and specifically how it relates to the student's experience with math. Three other procedural steps to be explored are (1) overview of irrational assumptions, (2) analysis of students' problem in rational terms, and (3) teaching the student to modify the statements she makes to herself.

Students keep a self-study chart in which negative feelings and antecedent events are recorded. Behavioral homework assignments are given as needed. Underscored throughout the sessions are the links between the cognitive, affective, and performance states. The discussion of psychological homework and sharing of biographical material are integral to the discovery of attitudes they hold around their identity and status as women. In each session there is at least one focus person in the group. It was significant that it is the stimulus of "math-related behavioral deficits" that gave rise to feminist issues.

WORKSHOP EVALUATION PROCESS

Post-workshop assessments were administered to determine attitudinal and behavioral changes. Instruments utilized in pre–post initial screening were the Math Anxiety Rating Scale (MARS), State-Trait Anxiety Inventory (STAI), Horner's Motive to Avoid Success(MAS), and Bem's Sex Role Inventory (SRI). Interrater reliability was established for observer measures of tensional manifestations. Data collected from workshop leaders, observers, and/or recorders were coded and statistically analyzed.

Exit interviews were held in which checklists and open-ended questions dealing with attitudes toward math, feelings of confidence toward math, and liking for math and math-related subjects were assessed. Group members were invited to evaluate the math workshops, the workshop leaders, the peer group, and the psychological techniques. In general, self-evaluation was encouraged.

A three-month follow-up interview was scheduled. The purpose was to determine the consistency, stability, and the direction of changes related to the math workshops. All interviews were conducted by adult women students who had not participated in this project.

RESULTS OF THE MATH-ANXIETY WORKSHOPS

A statistical analysis reevaluating data from workshop participants confirmed our observation that significant changes had occurred in a variety of ways. Anxiety scores were reduced in both mathematics and math-related situations. In addition to changes in MAS scores, rating scales, and observational reports, the Bem Sex-Role Inventory reflected a shift in the direction of androgyny. There was an increased liking for math and a greater feeling of confidence. Women were rejecting notions of math as a "male domain" and other stereotypes, and acknowledged the usefulness of math in today's job market. During the interviews, members reported increased self-esteem and self-understanding. Coping techniques were utilized in non-math situations as well. Alternate career options were now considered.

Reduction of math-anxiety behavior was maintained, as confirmed by a three-month follow-up study. Enrollment for mathematics courses increased. Postponement of math proficiency exams stopped. Students who took the tests passed. Students reported considerable tension decrease when confronting courses such as statistics, accounting, medical dosage, and introduction to computers. Observed tensional manifestations showed significant decrements throughout the workshop sessions. Workshop leaders who were non-math anxious revealed attitudinal shifts in Bem Sex Role Inventory and Horner's "Motive to Avoid Success." In short, evidence supported the reduction of math anxiety and math-avoidance behavior and increased confidence. These findings are consistent with those reported by Auslander[10] and Brush (1980); Fennema and Sherman (1978).

In the three-month follow-up session, as evidence of the stability of those changes, students spoke of their motivation around math and related areas. They reported maintaining friendships with other workshop members. They told interviewers they held a more positive self-concept and a raised level of consciousness about female competence.

IMPLICATIONS OF THE MATH ANXIETY WORKSHOPS

In assessing those factors most responsible for the remarkable shifts in their attitudes and behavior toward math, the feminist approach was felt to be an integral aspect of the process, enhancing the utilization of the psychological interventions. It was the gestalt of women working with women. The significance and stability of the changes noted must be attributable to the interactive effects of all aspects of the treatment package.

Several women continued to meet as a support group throughout the examination period and the subsequent semester. Participants in the original workshops enjoyed greater flexibility in their course selection.

10. Auslander, *op. cit*.

Some were pursuing "nontraditional" career goals. Half of the participants had made the Dean's List and received some form of merit scholarship. The momentum of this project helped create informal women's advocacy groups on campus. Intellectual stimulation, academic achievement, and nontraditional career goals were regarded as appropriate priorities in their lives.

During group discussion sessions feminist issues were raised. Each member examined in a very personal way in-depth patterns of sex-role stereotyping, role conflicts, relationships to significant others, and their own identity. In short, women defined who they were, what they wanted, and how they could handle more effectively the tasks leading to their goals. This was especially true for those who were the first in their family to attend college. Older adult students were, in effect, demanding to be taken seriously by family, friends, and faculty.

Another perspective helpful to understanding those women who experienced math anxiety is to apply the model of "learned helplessness" (Seligman, 1978). Throughout the workshop sessions, many members expressed feelings of powerlessness in controlling or mastering events and reactions related to math and other quantitative situations. These feelings generated anxiety and depression. Although avoidant behavior developed to what was felt to be so overwhelmingly threatening, the underlying sense was "I feel helpless, hopeless, and completely defenseless in the face of this Math Monster." Group sessions provided the students with the opportunity to reach this level of awareness. This consciousness was also the framework for relating to issues of feminism.

The success of a nontutorial intervention program provides an effective method to challenge and change those attitudes and behaviors that interfere with women taking control over their lives. Because the ninth year of secondary education reflects the emergence of sex differences in math performance, and the tenth year reveals patterns of math course enrollment differences between the sexes, a project such as this would be extremely valuable. Junior and senior high schools would be target places for introducing it. Of course teachers can perpetuate "math stereotypes" and significantly contribute to their own math anxiety and that of others. Therefore, workshops such as this designed for teachers, as well as students in primary and older grades, would have substantial impact. Federal and state mandates for more vigorous curriculum requirements in math and science point to the value of increased supportive measures to implement the shifts in standards.

The combination of both cognitive and behavioral approaches could also be applied to other areas of academic anxiety such as public speaking, science anxiety, test anxiety, writing anxiety, and computer anxiety. It is also essential for training in self-assertion and in survival skills in academe.

REFERENCES

Afflack, R. Mathophobia, a mini-course for the mathophobic. In J. Jacobs (Ed.), *Perspectives on women and mathematics*. ERIC Clearinghouse for Science, Mathematics and Environmental Education, 1978, pp. 73–101.

Aiken, L. R. Update on attitudes and other affective variables in learning mathematics. *Review of Educational Research*, 1976, *46* (2), 293–311.

Aldrich, M. Women and mathematics: Percent programs. Paper presented at *American Education Research Association*, March 1982, New York.

Bem, S. L. The measurement of psychological androgeny. *Journal of Consulting and Clinical Psychology*, 1974, *42*, 155–162.

Bem, S. L., & Lenney, E. Sex typing and the avoidance of cross-sex behavior. *Journal of Personality and Social Psychology*, 1976, *33* (1), 48–54.

Benbow, C., & Stanley, J. Sex differences in mathematical ability: Fact or artifact? *Science*, 1980, *210*, 1262–1263.

Betz, N. Prevalence, distribution and correlates of math anxiety in college students. *Journal of Counseling Psychology*, 1978, *25* (5), 441–448.

Boswell, S. L. "Nice girls don't study mathematics." Final report to the National Institute of Education. Boulder, Colorado, Institute of Research and Social Problems, January 1980.

Brush, L. *Mathematics and girls: The problem and the solution*. Cambridge, Mass.: Abt Associates, 1980.

Caballero, M., Giles, P., & Shaver, P. Sex role traditionalism and fear of success. *Sex Roles*, 1975, *1* (4), 319–326.

Carnegie Commission on Higher Education. *Opportunities for women in higher education*. New York: McGraw-Hill, 1973.

Casserly, P. L. *Assessment of factors affecting female participation in advanced placement programs in mathematics, physics and chemistry*. Princeton: Educational Testing Service, 1975.

Eccles (Pasons), J. Sex differences in math achievement and course enrollment. New York: American Educational Research Association, March 1982.

Ellis, A., & Grieger, R. *Handbook of rational-emotive therapy*. New York: Springer, 1977.

Ernest, J. Sex, sexism and anxiety in mathematics. In J. Jacobs (Ed.), *Perspectives on women and mathematics*. ERIC Clearinghouse for Science, Mathematics and Environmental Education, 1978.

Federbush, M. The sex problems of math school books. In J. Stacy, S. Bereand, & J. Daniels (Eds.), *And Jill came tumbling after: Sexism in American education*. New York: Dell Publishing, 1974.

Fennema, E., & Sherman, J. Sex-related differences in mathematics achievement, spatial visualization and affective factors. *American Educational Research Journal*, 1977, *14*, 51–71a.

Fennema, E., & Sherman, J. Sex-related differences in mathematics achievement and related factors: A further study. *Journal for Research in Mathematics Education*, 1978, *9*, (3), 189–204.

Fox, L., Brody, L., & Tobin, D. (Eds.). *Women and the mathematical mystique*. Baltimore: Johns Hopkins University Press, 1980.

Fox, L. *The problem of women and mathematics*. Report to the Ford Foundation, 1980.

Helson, R. Women mathematicians and the creative pesonality. *Journal of Consulting and Clinical Psychology*, 1971, *36*, 210–220.

Kaminski, D., Erikson, E., Ross, M., & Bradfield, L. Why females don't like mathematics: The effects of parental expectations. ERIC Document Reproduction Service No. Ed 154530, 1976.

Kreinberg, J. *Furthering the mathematical competency of women*. Public Affairs Report. Berkeley: University of California, 1976, Vol. 17, No. 6.

Kvarnes, R. Anxiety and math anxiety. In B. Donady & S. Auslander (Eds.), *Resource manual for counselors/mathematics instructors*. Washington, D.C.: Institute for the Study of Anxiety in Learning, 1980.

Lazarus, M. Rx for mathophobia. *Saturday Review of Literature*, June 28, 1975, 46–48.

Lazarus, M. *Self help kit for students: Math anxiety, math avoidance, reentry mathematics*. Washington, D.C.: Institute for the Study of Anxiety in Learning, 1980.

Liff, R. M. Programs to combat math avoidance. In J. Jacobs (Ed.), *Perspectives on women and mathematics*. ERIC Clearinghouse for Science, Mathematics and Environmental Education, 1978.

McLure, G. T., & Piel, E. College-bound girls and science courses: Perceptions of barriers and facilitating factors. *Journal of Vocational Behavior*, 1978, *12*, 178–183.

Mezirow, J., & Marsick, V. *Education for perspective transformation*. (Women's reentry programs in community college.) Center for Adult Education. New York: Columbia University, 1978.

National Research Council. *Summary Report 1981: Doctoral recipients from United States universities*. Washington, D.C.: Office of Scientific and Engineering Personnel, 1981.

National Center for Education Statistics. *Digest of Education Statistics*, 1979.

Nibbelink, W., & Mangru, M. Sexism in mathematics textbooks. In J. Jacobs (Ed.),

Perspectives on women and mathematics. ERIC Clearinghouse for Mathematics, Science and Environmental Education, 1978.

Parsons, J., Ruble, D., Hodges, K., & Small, A. Cognitive development factors in emerging sex differences in achievement-related experiences. *Journal of Social Issues*, 1976, 32 (3), 47–61.

Patty, R. A., & Stafford, S. F. Motive to avoid success, motive to avoid failure, state-trait anxiety and performance. In C. D. Spielberger & I. G. Sarason (Eds.), *Stress and anxiety: IV*. Washington, D.C.: Hemisphere, 1978.

Project on the Status and Education of Women. *The classroom climate: A chilly one for women?* Washington, D.C.: Association of American Colleges, Feb. 1982.

Resnick, H., Viehe, J., & Segal, S. Is math anxiety a local phenomenon? A study of prevalence and dimensionality. *Journal of Counseling Psychology*, 1982, 29 (1), 39–47.

Richardson, F. L., & Suinn, R. M. The mathematics anxiety rating scale: Psychometric data. *Journal of Counseling Psychology*, 1972, 19 (6), 551–554.

Rogers, R., & Craighead, W. E. Physiological responses to self-statements. The effects of statement valence and discrepancy. *Cognitive Therapy and Research*, 1977, 1 (2), 99–119.

Schlossberg, W. K., & Pietrofesa, J. J. Perspectives on counselors bias: Implications for counselor education. *The Counseling Psychologist*, 1974, 4 (1), 44–54.

Seligman, M. E. *Helplessness*. San Francisco: Freeman & Co., 1978.

Sells, L. W. The mathematics filter and the education of women and minorities. In L. Fox, L. Brody, & D. Tobin (Eds.), *Women and the mathematical mystique*. Baltimore: Johns Hopkins University Press, 1980.

Sherman, J. Social values, femininity and the development of female competence. *Journal of Social Issues*, 1976, 32 (3), 181–195.

Suinn, R. L. *Mathematics anxiety rating scale*. Fort Collins, Colorado: F. L. Collins Co., Rocky Mountain Behavioral Science Institute, 1972.

Tobias, S. *Overcoming math anxiety*. New York: Dial Press, 1978.

Tobias, S., Donady, D., & Kogelman, S. Math anxiety and female mental health: Some unexpected links. In C. Heckerman (Ed.), *The evolving female: Psychosocial perspectives*. New York: Human Services Press, 1979.

Walen, S., DiGiuseppi, R., & Wessler, R. *A practitioners guide to rational-emotive therapy*. New York: Oxford University Press, 1980.

Wolfe, J., & Fodor, I. A cognitive/behavioral approach to modifying assertive behavior in women. *The Counseling Psychologist*, 1975, 5 (4), 45–52.

Wolpe, J., & Lazarus, A. A. *Behavior Therapy techniques*. Oxford, England: Pergamon Press, 1966; 2nd Edition. New York: Pergamon Press, 1973.

■13

Some Feminist Concerns in an Age of Networking

DEBRA R. KAUFMAN

As final copy of this chapter was to be retyped, a colleague of mine who knew that I was writing about networking brought to my attention an article in that day's *Boston Globe*. There, just above an article entitled, "Science Closer to the Secrets of Longer Life" was the headline, "Rubin's New Revolution: Networking." The erstwhile Yippie, Jerry Rubin, had discovered networking. I immediately recomposed this introductory paragraph: for if networking had reached Studio 54, the mid-Manhattan discotheque, now a business networking salon owned by Jerry Rubin, one did not have to belabor the point that networking, both as method and metaphor,[1] had hit an all-time popular high. Rubin's message is clear: Contacts—who you know—can change your life. Networking has become a metaphor for the pathway to power based on the patterns of American males. And what about women in this milieu? Rubin claims that in his "business networking salon" women are treated as professionals and busi-

---

1. The use of networking as both method and metaphor was borrowed from the title of Barry Wellman's working paper "Network Analysis: From Method and Metaphor to Theory and Substance." The paper was listed among the working paper series of the structural analysis program brochure (August 1982), Department of Sociology, University of Toronto, 563 Spadina Avenue, Toronto, Canada, M55 1R1.

ness people—talking business, exchanging ideas, and making those all-important contacts (*The Boston Globe*, Monday, January 3, 1983, p. 34).

Although particularly popular over the past two decades, the term *networking* has been in the lexicon of many disciplines for several decades. Because networks are the ties among the different spheres of an individual's social world, they have been of particular interest to those working and writing in the social sciences. As Kadushin suggests, networks are dynamic systems with one or more of the following flowing through them: objects, labor, affect, evaluation, knowledge, prescription and opinion, influence, and power. Networks can be formal and informal (Kadushin, cited in Koenig & Gogel, 1981). Networks have been used not only to locate jobs and to advance one's career and occupational goals but to locate pediatricians, child care, care for the elderly, automobile mechanics, friends, lovers, as well as emotional and psychological support. Laura Lein (1983) has noted the many ways in which networks can be used among the poor, black communities, and the elderly. In fact, networks have been studied not only as interpersonal community ties but as interlocking corporate directorates and the world economic order; network analysis comprises sophisticated methodologies and computer programs as well as theories of class and property relations.

In most of the current research and literature the term has been used in the most narrow career sense, particularly in relation to women. For instance, in their advice to women wishing to become executives, Hennig and Jardim (1978) counsel women, not only to have a definite five-year plan for the kind of job they want, but also to determine the kind of people they will need to know to reach that goal, what these people can do to help them, and whom those people know.

However, research has not yet provided conclusive evidence that networking for this purpose yields the results it promises. Speizer, for instance, recounts some of the methodological problems with existing mentor studies: "1) The numbers are too small to allow one to generalize from the findings. 2) The information collected is retrospective. 3) The concepts of mentor or sponsor are left undefined" (1981, p. 711). In fact, the results of such networking might even have deleterious effects on women. One must remember that networks may be not only a source of support and opportunities for individuals but also a source of demands and constraints. Lein (1983) notes that gossip, ostracism, and withdrawal of support can be used as methods of keeping individuals in line with conventional behavior. Koenig and Gogel (1981) note that such covert network actions as group gossip, friendly advice, and informal decision making can be as powerful as overt economic force.

Networking, like its many synonymous terms—mentor, patron, sponsor, guide, godfather, and even rabbi—are generally used as metaphors for a process that lacks uniform operational definitions. Without clear definitions, the real effects of networking or the feminist implications of such a process have not been clearly understood or made explicit.

NETWORKING AND UPWARD MOBILITY:
MENTORS AND PROTEGES

Speizer (1981) notes that male business executives have provided the data which has led to the recommendation that women acquire mentors. But some important issues are left unexamined if we blindly follow such tutelege. Does becoming a protégée also mean assuming the mentor's values? If, as is still the case in the most prestigious professions, such mentors are male, does it also mean accepting the male-oriented competitive achievement values generally associated with such mentors? A 1979 *Wall Street Journal* article reported that 70 percent of women's mentors were male (*Wall Street Journal*, January 16, 1979, p. 1). Many writers have acknowledged that to be accepted into the informal social circles important for upward mobility in the professions, one must become socially similar to those at the top—simulating similar life styles, mannerisms, and, most importantly, aspirations and values (Epstein, 1970; Hughes, 1945; Kanter, 1977; Kaufman, 1977). Bringing women into positions of leadership and authority through the current male-dominated network may simply mean the perpetuation of the current systems of authority and leadership. Most of those who currently serve as mentors are not particularly positive regarding women.

For instance, in Bass, Krusell, and Alexander's (1971) study, 174 male managers and staff personnel perceived women as unable to supervise men and less dependable than men. In a more current study of managers' perceptions of sex differences, particularly perceptions relevant to the promotion of women, Rosen and Jerdee (1978, p. 841) found that male managers and administrators uniformly held more negative perceptions of women compared with men on each of four scales: aptitudes, knowledge, skills; interest and motivation; temperament; work habits and attitudes. Generally, women were perceived as having aptitudes, skills, interests, and motivations compatible with routine clerical roles, but not managerial ones.

Even in professions outside the world of business, such as academe, there are costs to be paid for mobility through male-dominated networks. Roger Collins[2] reflects on the concept of mentoring with regard to minority members and women academics. He concludes that to be a protégée, one has to be willing to ascribe to the social and intellectual legacy of the prospective mentor. The sex-biased nature of many of the intellectual theories and methodologies which structure our academic disciplines has been a feminist concern for well over a decade. Bringing women into positions of leadership and authority through a male filter may be too high a price for "making it."

Even if we were to hypothesize that women would bring a different sensibility once in positions of power (a very untested and unlikely hypothesis, especially if they ascend through male networks) the means to such ends may not be justified. For as Collins points out, mentors by definition are scarce and, as such, when potential mentees vie for scarce mentors, they undermine cooperative networking among themselves. As Laws (1975) pointed out when writing about the female token some years ago, in order to be one of the boys, the token occasionally must turn against the girls. Collins concludes that the intense competition generated among peers and an adherence to traditional belief systems "is analogous to colonialist strategies that require the colonized to abdicate their identity, their history, and their commitment to oppressed compatriots in order to receive colonial favors apparently crucial to their survival. The costs of establishing a professional identity forged in such a context needs to be acknowledged and assessed" (1982, p. 8).

WOMEN'S NETWORKS: TOWARD WHAT END?

Even if we were to agree with the commonsense but untested belief that mentoring or sponsorship is important for those on the rise, the mentoring process often embodies antithetical values to feminist sensibilities. Shapiro, Haseltine, and Rowe (1978) catalogue a list of problems associated with the mentor–mentee relationship. Do the very few women available as mentors or even role-models represent adequate or even appropriate female models from which we would want to build female networks? Even

2. Collins, R. Colonialism on campus: A critique of mentoring to achieve equity in higher education. Paper delivered to American Educational Research Association, March 19, 1982, New York.

if we had potential mentors and role-models, do we wish to imitate the hierarchical relationships implicit in any mentor–mentee relationship? Do we wish to imitate the intense, parental-like, if not patriarchal, quality of the relationship?

Mentoring would clearly have to change if we were to allay some feminist concerns about hierarchical relationships. Currently, the mentor–mentee relationship is not only socially restrictive but restricted in number as well. The attitudes, behavior, and personality characteristics currently valued in the male-dominated circles at the top do not allow for the diversity and alternative styles associated with what I have come to believe is a feminist model of success and professionalism—a style characterized more by cooperation than competition; more by teamwork than individualism; more by diversity than conformity; more by commitment to long-term effects than to short-term gains.

Many authors who offer critiques of the mentoring system have also offered suggestions for changing it. For instance, Shapiro et al. focus on the peer-pal or guide aspects of networking and mentoring. Using one's peers or those slightly higher in rank represents one way of learning the rules of the game while keeping the context more egalitarian. They argue that since there are more peers or persons closer in rank to new professionals, more mentoring can take place. Given each generation's changing needs, the authors suggest that new professionals need both men and women as "partial role models" in order to create "for themselves a composite ideal that represents the kind of professional toward which they aspire" (Shapiro et al., 1978, p. 54). In this way an aspiring professional can actively create (not passively accept) a role model for him/herself. In this way each can actively pick and choose the best qualities from each sex to carry him or her upward.

Collins (1982), too, argues for peer networking. He believes such alliances, particularly across institutions, are likely to provide members with a power base and access to more resources than would be available to any one individual. In fact, Collins argues that universities should pro- vide opportunities for networking among minority and women faculty by offering resources for junior faculty to establish and maintain professional contacts, especially ones outside of the university. However, the overriding belief in our culture that individual achievement depends on individual motivation and hard work makes this cooperative approach to achievement in times of scarce resources highly unlikely. Given current conditions, it is far more likely that a well-placed mentor can muster more resources than can peer-pals.

Furthermore, there are perils associated with these "new order" networks even if we avoid some of the pitfalls of the established "old-boy" networks. While the motives for peer networking or for establishing women's networks may be quite good, they may ultimately deflect women from changing current conditions or keep women peripheral to the real centers of power. In a recent *New York Times* magazine article, Anna Quindlen (1980) characterizes some of the motives behind what she calls the clear growth and direction of networks in the 1980s.

> The networks are for women who are anxious to help others of their sex but who are unabashed about their own desire to advance. They are for women who feel secure enough to move forward but still have some lingering doubts about their progress and position that are best assuaged by others in their situation. They are for women whose feminism, if it can be called that, is often more social than political. They are for women who work with and have contacts with men but who are not sure those men are willing to recommend or guide them. Above all, they are for women who feel there are services, insights, and assistance that other women can offer that are different, even better, than those that men could provide. They are job markets and support groups, lecture clubs and lobbying organizations. Some are connections based on professional status, race, or home town. All, of course, are connections based on gender (p. 86).

Although women's networks may be different, perhaps even better than the support men provide for one another, it is important to examine the political implications of such female support. If women's networks are more social than political, as Quindlen implies, will "networked" women address the current economic, political, and social inequality that affects women? If old girl networks are composed of women who have already "made it", usually through old-boy networks, will these successful women work to create access for other women, or simply enjoy the comfort of achievement? Will new networks seriously challenge society's dominant views about women's worth, or merely by providing the illusion of change, serve inadvertently to delay women's access to the significant centers of power?

Indeed, closer inspection of at least two of the most prestigious women's networks described in Quindlen's article leaves one unsure about just what it is that can be accomplished through networking. The women interviewed in Quindlen's article hypothesized that much good came from their mutual association, but they also admitted that they could not specify the exact consequences of such networking. Furthermore, Quindlen notes that by the time women might be nominated to join the prestigious Women's Media Group (a group limited to 140 members) or the Women's Forum, they probably do not need the support mechanisms such networks are thought to supply. For these women, learning the ropes or devising alternative strategies to open opportunities are not as important as simply relaxing in the company of other women. While such comfortability may provide a relaxed informal atmosphere, it might also provide a false sense of change and overall accomplishment. While such networks may bear some similarities to men's networks, they surely should not be construed as equal to those of men. Jane Gould, the director of the Women's Center at Barnard College, notes that although members of several women's networks were asked by the Reagan administration to recommend women for government positions, the high-ranking positions went to those women who were part of the most powerful men's networks (cited in Quindlen, p. 100). Gould warns in this same article that until we have many more women in decision making roles, we will not gain from networking what men gain (p. 100). She does not deny that the support we can give one another is a wonderful thing, but she cautions with the following: "I don't think anyone should fool themselves that because they know the 100 most powerful women in America, they know the 100 most powerful people" (p. 100).

Indeed my own study of academic women provided some similar data. The women I interviewed had markedly different colleague networks than men. The composition of their networks differed from that of men, with women having access to fewer colleagues in decision-making roles than did men. Their networks also served different purposes. Males used their colleagues more for professional contacts and less for friendship support than did women (Kaufman, 1978).

If we remain in separate networks from men, we may also remain isolated from the arenas wherein change can take place. I am not arguing that women's networks are not valuable. Networking among women can be a very important strategy and a potentially powerful force in boosting our own self-image. Networks can provide some important sources of information and help raise, to a public level, inequities once suffered as personal and as individual problems. But it is not a panacea for all of women's (or for that matter anyone's) political, social, and economic ills (for a more detailed account of women's current professional status, see Kaufman, 1983). What might be most damaging about separate networking for men and women is that separate networks might serve to emphasize rather than integrate feminine values into the corporate or professional culture. We must come to know our strengths and values not as different from men's (for then men become the norm) but as normative guides for human behavior. Our sensibilities must be valued by more than women in their networks—by the population at large. Networking is not enough unless we can collectively change existing institutions and the powerful bonds that maintain the status quo.

REFERENCES

Bass, B. M., Krusell, J., & Alexander, R. A., Male manager's attitudes toward working women. *American Behavioral Scientist*, 1971, *15*, 221–236.

Epstein, C. Encountering the male establishment: Sex status limits on women's careers in the professions. *American Journal of Sociology*, 1970, 75, 965–982.

Hennig, M., & A. Jardim. *The managerial woman*. New York: Pocket Books, 1978.

Hughes, E. Dilemmas and contradictions of status. *American Journal of Sociology*, 1945, *50*, 353–359.

Kanter, R. *Men and women of the corporation*. New York: Basic Books, 1977.

Kaufman, D. Women and the professions: Can what's preached be practiced? *Soundings*, Winter, 1977, *LX* (4), 410–427.

Kaufman, D. Associational ties in academe: Some male and female differences. *Journal of Sex Roles*, February, 1978, 5 (1), 9–21.

Kaufman, D. *Professional women: How real are the recent gains?* In J. Freeman (Ed.), *Women: A feminist perspective*. Palo Alto, Calif.: Mayfield, (forthcoming) 1983.

Koenig, T., & R. Gogel. Interlocking corporate directorships as a social network. *The American Journal of Economics and Sociology*, Jan. 1981, *40* (1), 37–50.

Laws, J. L. The psychology of tokenism: An analysis. *Sex Roles*, 1975, *1*, 51–67.

Lein, L. The ties that bind: An introduction to men's and women's social networks. In L. Lein & M. Sussman (Eds.), Special issue of *Marriage and Family Review*, (forthcoming) 1983.

Quindlen, A. Women's networks come of age. *The New York Times Magazine*, November 22, 1981, pp. 82, 100.

Rosen, B., & Jerdee, T. Perceived sex differences in managerially relevant characteristics. *Sex Roles*, 1978, *4*, 837–843.

Shapiro, E., Haseltine, F., & Rowe, M. Moving up: Role models, mentors, and the "patron system." *Sloan Management Review*, Spring 1978, 51–57.

Speizer, J. Role models, mentors, and sponsors: The elusive concepts. *Signs*, Summer 1981, *6* (4), 692–712.

INDEX

INDEX